Loss
Change
and Grief

An Educational Perspective

Erica Brown

Loss, Change and Grief

An Educational Perspective

Erica Brown

David Fulton Publishers
London

David Fulton Publishers Ltd,
Ormond House, 26–27 Boswell Street, London WC1N 3JD

First published in Great Britain by David Fulton Publishers 1999

British Library Cataloguing in Publication Data

A catalogue record for this book is available from the British Library

ISBN 1–85346–465–1

Typeset by FSH Ltd, London
Printed in Great Britain by The Cromwell Press Ltd, Trowbridge, Wilts.

Contents

This book is dedicated to
my grandchildren and godchildren
with my love

Foreword

Until the early years of the twentieth century, death, and particularly the death of children, was a part of everyday life. Since then, a very real taboo has developed around an issue which is the only certainty of life itself. Today in western society, the advances of medical science enable many life-threatened and life-limited children to enjoy a quality of life. Since 1969 the hospice movement has attempted to understand practical issues of care, and more recently children's hospices have played an increasing role in our understanding of how to meet the unique needs of each family without intruding.

As we approach the millennium we are entering into an age which demands trust, honesty and openness from all those who are concerned with working with families and children whose life experience causes them to encounter loss, change and grief.

This book is more than a comprehensive guide for all who strive to provide compassion and understanding as they help children and support the adults who care for them. The issues addressed are diverse and complex. We are challenged to face the taboo of death and dying as well as the myriad of individual circumstances which can lead to loss and grief. Within the realms of medicine, care services and schooling we are encouraged to develop professional capacities and integrity which extend beyond boundaries of faith and culture. Erica Brown writes sensitively and from her personal experience, yet in a practical way which brings together specific examples and documented interpretations.

Above all, this is a book which will truly support families who are living their lives in the shadow of death, since Erica has generously offered to donate all the royalties from sales to the CHASE Children's Hospice Service.

John L. Overton
Chief Executive
Acorns Children's Hospice Trust

Introduction

No mortal has ever pierced the veil of the great mystery of death. Yet, we have the inescapable responsibility to share with our children the fragments of our experience and knowledge. Grollman.

The classroom door burst open and the two seven year old children rushed up to where I was mixing paint for the afternoon art lesson. 'Jessica's Dad got squashed by a dustbin lorry. He's dead and her Gran is coming to tell you.' I barely had time to respond to what I had been told before two huddled figures joined the three of us in the corner of the classroom. I asked the two messengers to go back to the playground and searched helplessly in the depths of my mind for something my teacher training must have taught me about such situations. I didn't find the answers then, nor in the remainder of that first year I was qualified as a teacher. Thirty years later, faced with the same scenario, I'm sure I would still feel ill-equipped, but at least I have a generous number of years' experience to my credit.

Within all our lives there are losses such as being born and weaning which are necessary aspects of growth and change. But there are also losses which do not happen to everyone. These may be called 'circumstantial losses'. They include situations such as family breakdown, homelessness, the death of a relative or friend, abuse, imprisonment and serious illness or injury. Some adverse experiences can have both immediate and long-term consequences for children. Perhaps the most damaging effects are those which are harmful to mother–child relationships, but there are numerous events in children's lives which may have potentially damaging physical, social and emotional consequences.

Children's life experiences are not a feature of National Curriculum Orders, but we continue to test the children against national norms, ignoring the way loss, change and grief may impact on their emotional well-being and individual achievement. The opening sentence of Tolstoy's novel, *Anna Karenina*, rings unquestionably true for many children. He writes, 'All happy families are alike, but an unhappy family is unhappy after its own fashion.' In other words, families may have shared experience of events, but the consequences will be unique to each person within the family unit. In writing this book I have attempted to reflect on children's understanding of events, their responses to what has happened, and to suggest ways in which adults

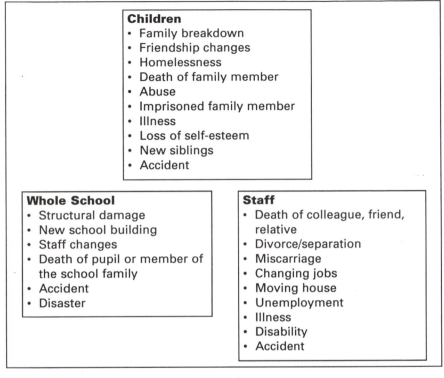

Figure 1 Circumstantial losses and changes

may support them. It has been necessary in many cases to make generalisations, but at the heart of the text is the individual child.

The right of children to have their views heard is of prime importance. This right extends to the area of research, and it is my belief that studies do not accurately or adequately represent the reality of children's experiences and responses unless some of their own accounts are take into consideration. Therefore, throughout the book, I will share short case studies with you. The quotations used are exactly as the children have told them to me, save for any names which have been changed to protect the anonymity of the young people concerned and their families.

Small-scale research findings on their own are unlikely to play a crucial role in educational policy-making or provision. However, the impact of the evidence may gradually enter into the thinking of policy makers and practitioners. It is my dearest hope that educators and support services will use the findings as a catalyst for their own imaginative initiatives.

Feelings and thoughts about death have always concerned people. Over the centuries poets, playwrights, novelists and authors have wrestled with the bittersweet experiences of living and dying. Most of us will have mixed feelings when we read accounts of children helping to lay out the bodies of their dead brothers and sisters at the beginning of the century. And there are scholars who have questioned the idealised view of death which pervaded Victorian Britain, claiming that the value of elaborate funerals was a commercial and ostentatious one rather than of any psychological benefit. But through being actively involved in the events which occurred after someone had died, our ancestors learned to view death as the natural progression of life. Death was 'accessible'. In many ways we have not replaced the practices of a hundred years ago with anything better. Most people die outside their homes. Hospitals take care of dead bodies, funeral directors lay them out and transport them and mourners become almost as lifeless as the corpse. Funerals are much more complicated occasions than weddings, yet nobody is given the opportunity of a rehearsal.

One of the earliest studies of adult grief took place in 1917 when Freud wrote a paper in which he described the mourning process and the differences between grief and depression (melancholia). Freud emphasised that normal grief was not an unhealthy condition. Just over half a century later, Bowlby endorsed Freud's theories of grief and extended his own thinking to consider that of children. He described powerful bonds of affection between children and their adult carers which are fundamental to feelings of well-being and safety. If the bond is broken or threatened, Bowlby believed this results in acute anxiety or grief. Bowlby went on to outline three phases of grief: protest, disorganisation and restructuring. The first phase is characterised by feelings of anger, disbelief, shock and yearning, and the child focuses his attention on thoughts of loss, crying and searching for the person who is no longer there. Bowlby's second phase is shown by despair, depression, withdrawal and social isolation. In the third phase the child is able to break away from the attachment, developing new interests and relationships, eventually returning to a level of functioning similar to that experienced before the loss.

Bowlby's work was extended by Kasterbaum (1977) who argued that it is how a young child experiences and attempts to come to terms with separation which contributes to their subsequent ideas of death. Finally, Anthony (1973) has given some of the most significant clues to children's early childhood fears about separation through death. She includes amongst her research findings vivid descriptions of children's sorrow and fear.

There are many types of bereavement and these give rise to different patterns of grief. Grief is the human response to loss and mourning is the way in which the grief is expressed. However the distinctions between grief and mourning are not clear-cut. Grief incorporates a myriad of emotional, behavioural (affective) and cognitive manifestations, both in adults and in children. Amongst the most traumatic events for children are the death of a parent, the death of a sibling, friend or peer, suicide or murder. Whatever the circumstances the death of the person is not only a loss, it is a turning point; the world will never be the same again.

It is beyond the scope of this book and my own expertise to attempt to give detailed accounts of the manifold causes and effects of grief in children. Although a qualified teacher, lecturer in Higher Education and a counsellor, I am not an expert. I do not know all the answers, because each grief carries with it a special burden about which my own experience may not qualify me to speak.

The first part of the book describes children's experiences and understanding of loss and change and discusses their emotional responses in relation to research and literature. Suggestions are given for how schools might cope when faced with a grieving child. The second part suggests how schools might provide a pastoral framework for caring for grieving children, as well as teaching about loss, change and death in the Religious Education Curriculum at Key Stages 1–3. I have discussed methods which I believe to be relevant to a variety of situations.

The text is not intended to provide guidance in the psychological theory of counselling children. It is first and foremost a practical text with practical ideas. Your own life experience or professional training may have taught you to interact with children and families in ways which are specific to their needs. Developing our own skills and capacities is good and it is impossible to provide guidelines which will fit every situation. Talking about loss, change and grief is a complex task. If we are haunted by feelings of death ourselves, children will sense our anxieties and tensions. Denying the reality of death can threaten to make our existence seem meaningless; acceptance can provide a bridge to span the abyss of our sorrow with those things which are most important to us. As we live through grief life goes on, and this is the hope which we can offer our children. Schools have rich opportunities to support children experiencing loss, change and grief through living out their stated ethos in practice. Additionally the pastoral curriculum and the Religious Education curriculum can enhance children's knowledge and understanding of other peoples' responses to life experiences.

The United Nations Convention of the Rights of the Child defines a child as someone under the age of eighteen. Throughout the book the words child, pupil and young people are used interchangeably to cover the chronological age ranges of those who might still be in full-time schooling. Rather than using combined personal pronouns such as s/he, his/hers, him/her, which are not congruous with the way in which we speak, I sometimes use personal pronouns which relate to the female gender and sometimes those which relate to the male. I also recognise that many adults act in caring roles or are part of extended families. Therefore the term 'parents' does not refer exclusively to biological parents.

In the course of writing I have drawn on the ideas, memories, advice and support of a great many people. Some are professionals kind enough to share their knowledge with me; others are people who have been brave enough to trust me and to share their stories. I never cease to be amazed by the courage and openness of families which has been both challenging and humbling. Their ability to survive in the face of adversity is an example to us all. I also acknowledge that playing a professional role takes its toll, and were it not for the support of my colleagues at Westminster College, the book would not have been completed. I am indebted to my dear friend and secretary Sally Lloyd who has painstakingly transcribed tape recordings and gave up some holiday to type the manuscript.

By far my greatest gratitude is to Alan, my husband, who has contributed to putting back together the pieces of my own life more than he will ever know. Throughout our marriage he has constantly and unselfishly made sacrifices so that I have been able to pursue personal and professional quests. To my (our) godchildren and grandchildren to whom this book is dedicated, I can only say with great affection and pride, 'thank you' for allowing me to 'learn on the job'. For my own daddy who died as I sat down to write this introduction, I am glad I had a last chance to thank you for your unconditional love.

A book is a platform for ideas and opinions. Inevitably my own views and life experiences are held between the covers. Because we are all different, the ways in which we cope in the face of adversity and the strategies which we adopt will be individual. There will be areas where your skills exceed my own. The guidelines are intended as a springboard for your own good practice.

There is no single way to support children who are grieving. Yet there are avenues open to each one of us. Keep travelling alongside those who hurt and listen to the words they use and be aware of the ways they choose to communicate. Pace yourself with the child and her family and be sensitive to people's own need to be active participants in what is happening. Always give your support, but do not intrude. Care, but do not lose sight of the emotional price which you pay for your own commitment. Seek solace, guidance and comfort for yourself. But most importantly, trust the children and their families to be your guides.

Chapter 1

Loss, Change and Grief in Children's Lives

Before the impact of loss and grief can be fully understood the meaning of *attachment* needs to be explored. Bowlby's (1969) attachment theory describes the tendency of people to establish affectional bonds with others and the grief response which occurs when these are threatened or severed. Bowlby's thesis argues that attachment comes from a human need for security and safety which is prevalent throughout life. However he sees attachment as extending beyond the physical needs of a young child (for example) for food, warmth and comfort. The quality of attachment determines the capacity of the child to establish affectional bonds later in life. More recent studies endorse Bowlby's theories citing the work of anthropologists throughout the world who speak of a universal attempt to regain lost objects and a grief response if this is denied.

Engel's (1961) and Klein's (1960) research argues that response to loss may result in physiological and psychological illness. Just as medicine and healing may be necessary to restore bodily well-being, a period of adjustment and adaptation to grief are necessary so that normal functions can take place.

More recent research suggests it is necessary that 'tasks of mourning' take place (Worden 1988, Parkes 1972a). These involve:

- accepting the reality of the loss;
- experiencing the pain of grief;
- adjusting to a new environment;
- investing in new relationships.

A number of researchers and practitioners argue that the tasks of mourning are not exclusively adult phenomena (Smith and Pennells 1995, Holland 1997, Herbert 1996, Dyregrov 1991). Studies in adult psychiatric patients have confirmed that loss and grief in early childhood can have a damaging effect Rutter 1966, Brown 1961). Moreover, a debate has emerged about post-traumatic stress disorder in children as young as eight years old following tragic and unexpected events (Dyregrov 1991, Couldrick 1991, Duffy 1991).

Some confusion in the debate on childhood grief arises from the fact that children's responses to grief may be shown differently from those of adults. How an individual copes with loss depends on a variety of factors, including previous life experience and the support systems that they have around them (Holland 1997). However the most common reactions are:

- shock and grief;
- sorrow and protest;
- numbness and disbelief;
- continuation of life.   Parkes (1972a)

Terr (1976) argues that there is a striking similarity between grief responses in children and in adults.

The stages described below are only guidelines. The feelings and reactions of children faced with loss and separation, whether through death or other causes, are manifold, and they reflect children's cultural, emotional and religious background (Black 1989, Brown 1997, Brown 1994).

Babyhood – toddler stage

Children in the very early years are at the beginning stages of developing their own sense of identity together with social, learning and life skills. They are still very largely dependent on adults and their understanding of crisis situations is determined by their life experience. It is thought that young children may have a higher sense of anxiety if they are separated from a primary carer. However, because of their age they seem to have difficulty in grasping the long-term implications of separation, believing the person who is no longer there is likely to return.

Duffy (1991) and Bending (1993) write of babies as young as six months old reacting to separation from their primary carers by showing irritability, erratic eating, sleeping and crying patterns. Dyregrov (1991) describes this group of children as being amongst the most 'helpless'. However he also believes they may be protected to a certain extent by their inability to grasp the long-term consequences of what has happened.

Early years

From the age of about two to five years children grow in independence although they are unable to grasp the permanence of separation and they demonstrate behaviour aimed at the restoration of an absent person or object (Couldrick 1991). A child who experiences the loss or death of a primary carer at this age will need help in understanding the irreversible nature of the situation. It is not uncommon for them to ask about the physical well-being of the dead person. However, their lack of understanding about the permanence of the situation may also account for a lack of reaction when learning about an event. Jane, aged four, had just been told of her baby brother's cot death when she asked 'Can I have an ice-cream yet?' Likewise Sabina, five years old, said she was going out to play and skipped off down the garden when the news of her Daddy's death in a car accident was told to her. Dyregrov (1991) agrees that generally such responses may reflect children's repertoire of coping strategies for grieving.

Children may regress in skills they have already acquired and their anger may be expressed through play (Harris-Hendricks *et al.* 1993). Some children will show physical malaise in response to their grief such as 'tummy ache' or 'head ache'. Very occasionally their symptoms may mirror those of a person who has died (Pennells and Smith 1995).

Seven to nine years

As intellectual capacity develops, so does children's imagination and during the middle years, it is not uncommon for youngsters to imagine they were responsible for separation or a death. However, they begin to demonstrate empathetic feelings towards others who have experienced losses (Dyregrov 1991). As children mature they become increasingly independent as they interact with a wider social circle outside their immediate families. They begin to form longer-lasting relationships with their peers and they are more in control of their emotions, developing coping strategies in crisis situations. Because their imagination develops rapidly this may shield them from anxiety if they believe that sadness can be reversed through 'magical' thought processes. When their life experience proves that separation is permanent they may develop extreme anxiety and even guilt, believing that they were responsible for the situation in which they find themselves.

Adolescence

Children's concept of death becomes more abstract and they understand more of the long-term consequences of loss (Dyregrov 1991). Increased cognitive capacity enables them to develop an awareness that death is common to all living things, that it is irreversible, universal and inevitable. This may in turn lead to a fear of their own mortality although Pennells and Smith (1995) suggests most youngsters 'get on with life'.

Characteristic physical and emotional changes of adolescence, combined with increasing independence, may lead to confusing and conflicting emotions especially about death and some young people have described feeling suicidal (Vander-Wyden 1991). Some children may express their feelings through exhibiting challenging behaviour (O'Brien 1998). During this age the 'magical' thinking of earlier childhood may be re-activated and feelings of remorse and self-blame are common. Because they are now able to think ahead to the future children may perceive the long-term consequences of separation. In addition, because young adults have learnt to control their emotions they may be afraid of any outward expression of grief, believing that they need to stay in control. Occasionally this may lead to a desire to control other people and the environment and they take risks in dangerous situations to prove themselves.

In summary, children's attempts to master what has happened is dependent on their age and maturity although there are some parallels across ages. Figure 1.1 summarises the sequence.

	Infant/Toddler	Key Stage 1	Key Stage 2	Adolescent
Cognitive Factors	• Onset of attachment at about 6 months after birth. • Permanence of absence or death not understood. • Ability to conceptualise the word 'death' very limited. • Children begin to incorporate small 'losses' into their lives. • Children are aware of the adult use of the word 'death'.	• Able to classify, order and quantify events and objects but unable to give a rationale. • Concept of 'life' and 'death' established e.g. death equals separation. • Understand the state of death means not breathing, not moving, still etc. • Permanence of death still not established. Stage of 'magical' thinking e.g. thoughts/actions may be responsible for death.	• Able to explain reasoning in a logical way. • Realisation that death can be applied to self. • Permanence of death established. • Death is understood as an ultimate reality. • Confusion about metaphors and euphemisms associated with death e.g. 'gone', 'asleep', 'lost'.	• Abstract thought patterns established. • Interest in physical characteristics of death and dying. • Questions asked How? Why? • Own theories about what happens at death and beyond formed. • Interest in ethical issues e.g. abortion, euthanasia.
Emotional Response	• Separation anxiety. • Yearning and searching for the person who is not there. • Expression of sadness short-lived. • Blame other people for death/departure. • Fantasises about the dead person – united with the dead person. • Rejection of affection from new primary carer.	• Excessive crying. • Unable to control emotions. • Poor concentration at school and play. • School refusal. • Illusions/hallucinations about the dead person – night terrors. • 'Play out' death and dying.	• Anxiety about other people dying. • Disturbance in normal behaviour patterns. • More in control of emotional responses. • Inability to organise and to concentrate. • Stealing objects as 'comfort'. • Capacity to sustain feelings of sadness for longer.	• Whole range of emotions displayed. • Feel embarrassed about being 'different'. • Anxiety about the future e.g. material possessions/economics • Inability to form new lasting relationships. • Rejection of affection from other people.
Physical Response	Children who have not developed verbal language may respond by: • bedwetting • wetting by day • viral infections • disturbed sleep.	• restlessness • loss of appetite • 'tummy-ache' psychosomatic illness • clinging behaviour • night terrors	• aggression • changed behaviour • nail biting • sleep disturbance • physical illness	• eating disorders • challenging behaviour • physical illness • disturbed sleep • conflict • risk-taking behaviour • increased sexual or permissive behaviour.

Figure 1.1 Children's cognitive, emotional and physical responses to death

The grief process

The process of grief does not progress through straightforward clearly defined stages beginning with the discovery of the loss and ending with the return to normal life. Various scholars describe different structures. At the beginning of the chapter we considered Worden's (1988) 'four tasks of mourning'. Parkes (1972a) uses a sequence of stages to describe adult grief which may usefully be applied to children, not least because there is a striking similarity between grief reactions in children and adults.

Anxiety

Because children are largely dependent on adults for their well-being, they can experience a tremendous sense of anxiety if their security is threatened. If a primary carer has died they may fear the loss of other adults in their lives and keep asking 'what will happen if?' Young children and toddlers may refuse to go to bed alone and want to keep adults in sight. Others may worry about finances, holiday arrangements etc. Occasionally children refuse to go to school feeling that if they are with adults they can make sure all is well at home.

> A four year old whose twin sister was life-threatened and went to a hospice for respite care once a month always complained of tummy ache on the Friday her twin was due to be away for the weekend. She seemed to need to make sure where her sister was going. After her parents started taking her with them when they dropped her twin at the hospice she was much happier and seemed to feel she was more in control.

Other children who have witnessed a death or tragedy may re-live the event and appear unable to relax. They may avoid the location where the incident happened, fearing the same thing could happen again or that the frightening range of emotions which they experienced might re-emerge. Where a child has experienced a cot death or the prolonged illness and death of a sibling, they may have a terror of pregnancy or young children.

What do children need?
- Reassurance that their world has not disintegrated.
- Information or honest answers to their questions.
- Patience and support from the people around them.
- Time to adjust to a new way of life.
- Routines and stability at home and school.
- Language which is straightforward and easily understood.
- Time to accept their emotions as well as time to express them.

Anger

Anger is frequently experienced by children after a loss and it can be a very confusing and frightening emotion. Often this is accompanied by physical aggression such as kicking or lashing out at other people. Alternatively it may be directed at themselves believing that they were in some way to blame for what happened, or at the person who is no longer there. Dyregrov (1988) believes anger is more commonly expressed by boys than girls. However this is not always the case:

> A ten year old girl was so angry her mother had died she used her chair to break every mirror in the house, repeating as she did so 'Now you can't ever, ever, ever look in here again'.

What do children need?
- A safe place to express their anger and confusion.
- Adults who are prepared to listen and who acknowledge their grief.
- Reassurance that they were not responsible for what happened.
- Time to adjust to what has happened.
- Familiar routines and life styles.
- Adults who will admit they don't know all the answers.

Denial and disbelief

The immediate response to bad news such as death is that it simply cannot be true. Whilst they are trying to adapt to the new situation most people have times when the reality is just too sad to bear so their consciousness lapses into the familiar 'known' world where the upsetting information does not need to be incorporated. Most deaths will cause an immediate grief response in children of shock and denial. Because they may feel numb and confused they revert to the security of their familiar surroundings and life style, often causing adults to wonder at their ability to carry on as if nothing had happened. Reality breaks in suddenly and may be triggered by an apparently trivial event.

> Kirsten, aged nine, had been told of her grandfather's death but had apparently shown no grief reaction. However, after the funeral, the school rabbit escaped and was killed by a fox. She dissolved into inconsolable tears saying it wasn't fair. God had not looked after the rabbit and He hadn't looked after her granddad either because he was dead.

What do children need?
- To be told the facts about what has happened as clearly and concisely as possible and in language which they understand.
- Familiar routines and safe surroundings.
- People who will help to keep the memory of the person 'alive'.
- To be allowed to express their responses in a way which is right for them as long as they are not endangering themselves or anyone else.

Vivid memories and night terrors

During grief it seems some people experience an altered state of consciousness in which 'sensory impressions are registered, processed and memorised in a manner different from the ordinary' (Dyregrov 1991). Later these images can come back in the form of memories or intrusive visions. Children who are pre-verbal are also able to experience this and later when verbal language develops they may be able to describe the images (Eth and Pynoos 1985).

> Michael, aged six, with a statement of special educational needs, had witnessed the sudden death of his grandmother. For several years after the event he would suddenly 'freeze' when he was near tall trees and, shaking in terror, he would point and sign that his grandmother's face was looking down at him. He also experienced nightmares and it was not until his early teens that he could be persuaded to pass trees.

Disturbed sleep is common. Many children will have heard adults use the euphemism 'sleep' to describe death, and this may lead to interrupted or disturbed sleep. They may be afraid of falling asleep in case they too die. Amy, aged five, had heard her parents talking about death as not breathing. One night she sobbed herself to sleep telling her mummy she might forget to breathe in the night. Dyregrov (1991) says children who do not explore their fears and anxieties about death during the day may do so at night.

What do children need?
- Language which describes death in a way which is understood.
- Reassurance that they are 'safe' as they sleep.
- Opportunities to act out or role-play their anxieties or experiences.
- Information and honest answers to their questions.

Sadness and longing

Young children seem to have a fairly short sadness span. Their sadness tends to be expressed in many different ways which range from bitter outbursts of crying to quiet withdrawal. It is not unusual for young children to wander from room to room in the house searching for the person that is 'lost'. Older children frequently try to protect the adults around them by concealing their grief and they may try to persuade adults that their sadness is for other reasons, for example minor injury. Others may role-play the dead person in an attempt to console family members (Jewett 1982).

Often children will require tangible things as comfort objects and they may hide things which belong to the person who is no longer there.

> Hayley, aged seven, refused to be parted from one of her dead big sister's sweaters for nearly ten months after she had died but she always hid it under the bed during the day hoping her parents would not find it.

What do children need?
- A 'safe place' to express their emotions.
- Opportunities to role-play their experiences and emotions.
- Continuity in care at home and at school.
- Adults who will comfort them and help them to express how they feel.

The separation experienced in bereavement is permanent and many children who are able to grasp the irreversible nature of the separation will feel a sense of remorse that they were in some way responsible for a situation which is out of their control. Collick (1985) describes this feeling of guilt as a 'universal emotion' effecting old and young alike.

For children imagined guilt or self-blame may lead to huge misery especially when it is combined in the early years with egocentric thought and magical thinking. Many will at some stage have wished a sibling or adult dead or even shouted 'drop dead' or been deeply jealous of a person. If the person becomes ill or dies, they may feel responsible. Some of the most commonly heard phrases are 'if only I had...' or 'if only I had not...' This reaction is known as 'survivor guilt'. If children are present at the time of death guilt feelings may be further exaggerated.

What do children need?
- Reassurance that they were not to blame either through thought or neglect.
- Time to adjust to what has happened.
- Opportunities to express their anxiety, for example through counselling or therapy.

Bowlby (1977) and Parkes (1972a) believe that the tasks of mourning are complete when the person has returned to the state she was in prior to the bereavement. Worden (1988) qualifies this by saying that the 'return' has no definitive time-scale. In many cases he believes the process takes up to two years, a fact which is supported by the example of Jenny whose father died in an accident at work when she was five and a half. It was not until just before her eighth birthday that she could be persuaded to abandon the idea that if she had not returned to school (after recovering from chicken-pox) on the day her Daddy died, she could have prevented the tragedy from happening.

Loss, change and grief in the lives of people with special educational needs

Except for the most profoundly handicapped, the response to bereavement and the process involved in trying to overcome loss are essentially the same as in people of normal intelligence. McLoughlin (1986).

Oswin (1991) writing nearly a decade ago says that in spite of the empowerment of people with learning disabilities within statutory education, 'it appears in the area of loss and bereavement they are still not receiving enough consideration, nor the appropriate support they require', (p. 26). The same author argues this shortfall is largely due to an assumption that people with learning disabilities do not experience the same emotional response to loss and grief as others do, and secondly the combination of a 'double taboo' of learning disabilities and 'death' has challenged society to the extent that they have been swept under the carpet. Furthermore, grief is often considered as part of abnormal behaviour associated with the learning disability rather than a human response.

Research into the development of the concept of death

Bihm and Elliot (1982) suggest that the concept of death in adults with special educational needs is akin to the concept of death in children as described by Piaget and cited earlier in this chapter. Piaget's model, based on the chronological age of the child, has however been challenged by scholars such as Bluebond-Langner (1989) who describes how very young children who are terminally ill or life-threatened have a sophisticated understanding of death through their observation of how adults respond, knowledge of their own symptoms and treatment and interaction with other dying children.

More recently the work of Speece and Brent (1984) concerning the conceptual understanding of death by people with special educational needs has been further developed by McEvoy (1989) who has found that the more able people with special educational needs are at communication skills, self help skills, and social development, the more advanced they are in their concept of death and dying. Kronick (1985) claims that in addition to needing abstract conceptual skills in order to understand death, a person also needs to possess concepts of time, space, causality, finality and separation.

The effects of bereavement and how people continue to adjust and lead their lives has been well documented (Brown and Harris 1989, Parkes 1972a, Parkes 1985). Research into how people with learning disabilities respond is however limited and in the main concentrates on people in long-term residential care (Oswin 1991, Strachan 1981). McLoughlin (1986) believes that people with learning disabilities are too often perceived as a homogeneous group with the result that their needs may be seen to be different than their mainstream peer group. Oswin (1981) supports this view, saying that problems experienced by bereaved persons who have learning disabilities are often the direct result of being treated differently from the norm. Sheila, a middle-aged lady with severe learning difficulties, told her mother who commented she thought she had seen her husband who had died a month before, 'Don't be stupid. He's gone for always and forever.'

Despite the similarities of grief responses among children and adults of all abilities described by authors such as McLoughlin (1986) it is however important to consider those which may be specific to people with special educational needs. Brelstaff's research (1984) found numerous differences between individuals and McEvoy (1989) indicates that past experience of death does not necessarily improve cognitive understanding of people with special educational needs.

The importance of allowing children time to grieve has already been described. French and Kuczaj (1992) believe society affords insufficient scope to allow people to grieve in a way which they feel necessary and that this shortfall includes people with special educational needs.

> When twenty-six year old Kevin was told his father had died he shouted at the clergyman who gave him the news and kept saying 'No, no.' Later he needed to be told again and again about his father's illness and how he was so ill nothing could be done to save his life. Generally after staff had given him these facts he would repeat over and over again that he had shouted at his father and it was therefore his fault that his dad had died.

What is significant about Kevin's story is that his responses are human ones. They are not specific to a man with cerebral palsy. He is angry, confused, disbelieves what has happened, needs to know all the details and feels guilty and that in some way he was responsible for what happened.

Turner and Graffam (1987) studied a group of people with learning disabilities who attended a day centre. The group were asked if they had experienced any dreams concerning death. A consistent theme was the appearance of the deceased person in dreams, often including an invitation to join them. Others dreamt about how the death had happened, especially in relation to accidents or sudden death. A feature of both types of dreams was a sense of helplessness reported by the people who had experienced them, a feature consistent with accounts by people with learning difficulties.

The following responses to bereavement by people with learning disabilities are common:

Emotional

- sadness
- anger
- disbelief
- shock

Physical

- digestive problems
- exhaustion
- sleep disorders
- incontinence

Cognitive

- denial
- hallucinations
- preoccupation with death
- confusion

Behavioural

- regression in previously mastered skills
- withdrawal
- searching
- over-sensitivity to noise
- self-injury.

Many people carry lonely burdens. But for people with special educational needs the emotional upheaval and confusion may be accepted as a natural result of their grief. Bereavement outcome depends on many factors such as support, opportunities to grieve, the circumstances of the death and the nature of the relationship with the deceased (Stroebe and Stroebe 1987). These differences are likely to apply to people with special educational needs as well as the general population. In addition there are number of inter-related factors which should be recognised within the context of working with bereaved persons with special educational needs. These are described in Figure 1.2, in the chart entitled 'Inter-relating features in bereavement'.

Caring for bereaved people

The work of Black (1989) suggests that the way in which people adjust to bereavement is largely due to how well the primary carers cope and how open

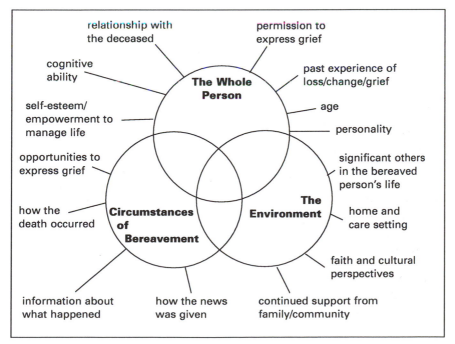

Figure 1.2 Inter-relating features in bereavement

the family are to the expression of grief. Furthermore, where a death is anticipated Lindsay *et al.* (1993) suggest that some work on helping clients develop coping strategies may be helpful.

Often professionals caring for people with limited communication skills mistakenly feel that they do not experience grief after a bereavement which Moddia (1995) writes may lead to a 'conspiracy of silence'. It has been suggested that the key to successful management of bereavement comes partly through non-verbal communication and understanding (Parkes 1985). Indeed, Oswin (1991) believes that the affectionate attachment may be more important than professional expertise.

Worden's (1988) four stages of grief based on Bowlby's attachment theory (discussed earlier in the book) are helpful in the context of people with special educational needs. The stages are:

- acceptance of the reality of the loss;
- working through grief;
- adapting to life without the deceased;
- investment in new relationships.

Accepting the reality of the loss

What do people need?
- Information about what happened in language which avoids metaphors and euphemisms.
- Help to person to understand 'dead' means not moving, not breathing, not living.
- Attending the funeral where possible.
- Having an opportunity to symbolise 'goodbye' – flowers, notes etc.
- Visiting the grave.

Working through the pain of grief

What do people need?
- Talking about/communicating feelings.
- Time to pace grief.
- Opportunities to maintain familiar routines.
- Experience of compassion from carers.
- Talking about how feelings have changed.

Adapting to life without the deceased

What do people need?
- Opportunities to keep the memory of the deceased alive.
- Time to grieve and to adjust.
- Opportunities to manage their lives.
- Naming significant other people they know.

- Maintaining contact with people who know about their likes and dislikes.
- Mementos and symbols to remember the deceased.
- Marking anniversaries etc. which were an important part of life before the bereavement.
- Opportunities to develop new interests.

Investing in new relationships

What do people need?
- Reminiscing about past times.
- Reminiscing about past relationships.
- Permission to enjoy life and to move on.

Breaking bad news

Breaking bad news is always an unenviable task but for those who have to do this to people with learning difficulties the process is likely to be even more stressful. At a time when emotions are running very high, skills are called upon which may never have been rehearsed, let alone developed. Perhaps the most important principle is not to withhold the news of the death but communicate what has happened to the bereaved person in language which they understand. Metaphors and euphemisms should be avoided since they are easily misunderstood or taken literally. Ideally the information should be given in a familiar place where the bereaved person feels safe and by a person she knows and trusts.

Meeting individual needs

The way in which bereaved people respond to the news of the death will be individual and dependent on factors such as their cognitive ability, age, life experience, faith or cultural background. The personality of the person will also effect their response which may vary from quiet withdrawal on one hand to bitter weeping and crying on the other. Figure 1.3 shows the response of one person with learning difficulties.

Sometimes coping strategies are imposed on people, a fact which James (1995) believes is damaging and detrimental. Generally the rule of thumb is to allow individual persons to respond to bad news in a way which is right for them and to encourage them to be patient in their grief. It is likely that a person's thoughts and attitudes will change over the course of the process. Therefore carers need to be aware that as the bereaved person attempts to come to terms with the loss, they may need to be supported in the process and helped to reach an acceptable conclusion. Anger, tears and apathy are normal human responses to grief and for people who do not have verbal communication skills carers will need to help them to express levels of emotional response.

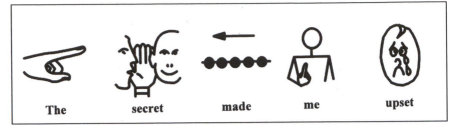

| The | secret | made | me | upset |

Figure 1.3 Thirty-five year old Hannah communicated the above to her carers when she discovered she had not been told about her mother's death (Source: author)

Families are an important resource during bereavement but their needs should not be overlooked since they too will be coming to terms with the loss. In supporting the person with special needs, the needs of significant persons in his or her life should also be considered.

Where bereaved persons have verbal language repetitive questions are a frequent response to loss. Seldom will the person need more information than they ask for. Therefore it is essential to answer the specific questions carefully. Gradually the queries may be replaced with memories of the dead person but Stein (1974) emphasises the importance of allowing repetitive queries to continue as long as the person wants.

All people will need time to adjust to an environment without the deceased person. This will often mean changed living circumstances, loss of affection, support and companionship. As Cynthia told her carer, 'For two years the drops did come from both my two eyes and run down my face.'

The work of Strachan (1981) and Oswin (1991) is seminal in the context of grief and bereavement for people with special educational needs in residential care settings. Strachan in particular has explored reactions to bereavement of residents in large institutions and the effects of experiencing multiple bereavements during long-term care. Oswin's observations are also useful especially concerning how people with learning disabilities may be denied time and privacy to grieve.

I remember meeting a lady who had been in residential care for twelve years after her mother died. Throughout those twelve years her grief had gone unrecognised by staff as she failed to adjust to her environment without ever understanding why she no longer lived at home. Her sole possession from her home was a cushion from which she refused to be parted. When she died herself two letters of condolence, one written when her father died twenty years before and one at the time of her mother's death, were found in her bedside drawer unopened. No one had thought to read them to her.

Even when grief is recognised, families and carers may be at a loss as to what they can do. The following guidelines do not pretend to be exhaustive. Neither will they be helpful in all residential settings.

Guidelines for when a person living in residential care dies

- Where a person is dying they should remain in familiar surroundings with familiar people caring for them.
- News of the death of a resident or member of staff should be shared with everybody concerned.
- Residents should be given opportunities to communicate their sadness.
- Residents should be able to see the body after death if they express a wish to do so and relatives do not object.
- Residents should be given opportunities to contribute flowers, condolences etc.
- Residents should be given the same opportunities as staff to attend the funeral.
- Immediate assessments or major decisions regarding the future of any residents should be avoided where possible.

Guidelines for when a relative of a person living in residential care dies

- The person should be told as soon as possible after the death.
- The person should be informed about the circumstances of the death.
- The bereaved person should be allowed to express their grief in any way they wish as long as their own safety or the safety of other people is not at risk.
- The bereaved person should be encouraged to ask as many questions as they wish.
- Questions should be answered as openly and honestly as possible.
- The bereaved person should be allowed to contribute to flowers, memorials etc., if they wish.
- The bereaved person should be allowed or encouraged to attend the funeral.
- The bereaved person should be given opportunities to visit the grave or the garden of remembrance especially at anniversaries etc.
- Opportunities should be given for the bereaved person to write thank you letters for condolences received, flowers etc. where appropriate.
- Staff should make themselves familiar with the faith or cultural background of all residents when they come to live in the home.
- Assessments or major decisions regarding the future of the bereaved person should be avoided where possible.
- All members of management and care staff should be informed as soon as the bereavement has occurred.
- Familiar routines of care should be maintained wherever possible.

Bereavement in school families

Schools are busy places and whilst they may be models of excellence in the daily care and education of their pupils, it is sad to recognise that many are in fact at a loss as to how to respond when a death occurs. Literature suggests there is a need for greater understanding and better support for bereaved people with learning difficulties (Kloppel and Hollins 1989, Yule and Gold 1993).

This lack of response may in part be due to:
- a lack of communication amongst staff;
- a lack of professional development or training;
- a lack of understanding concerning the way in which people with special educational need express their needs and express their grief;
- a sense of fear on behalf of carers and support staff.

Oswin (1991) believes that senior management are often less in touch with the way in which children with special educational needs express grief than their more junior counterparts or indeed care staff. Guidelines on school policies and frameworks for care will be considered later on in the book. However, it is important to recognise how children with special educational needs, particularly those with severe learning difficulties and those with profound and multiple learning difficulties, may respond when there is a bereavement in school. The following points were noted by teachers of pupils with severe learning difficulties and profound and multiple learning difficulties. They suggest that children in their classroom respond by:

- feeling alone and vulnerable;
- missing familiar environments and routines;
- being particularly sad at holiday times, festivals etc. which have been shared occasions;
- protecting other people from their sadness;
- losing weight;
- suffering digestive problems, loss of appetite or feeding problems;
- having disturbed sleep patterns and feeling physically tired;
- becoming fretful or regressive.

How can adults help children?
- Communicate understanding or responses of sadness and loss.
- Keep pictures or belongings which belonged to the deceased or anything which had a particular tactile or sensory quality.
- Visit familiar places.
- Keep routines as familiar as possible.
- Provide a safe environment.
- Avoid immediate admission to residential care after a death wherever possible.
- Ensure contact with familiar people who are consonant with preferences, likes or dislikes.

How one special school responded to the death of their head teacher

Mr Bigger was the head teacher of a large special school in the south of England. For a number of months he had complained of indigestion and stomach disorders and had been away from schools for short periods. He was a popular man and always encouraged pupils to visit him in his study to share their achievements. When he was not there he was generally to be found in the classroom taking an interest in everything which was going on. One day he collapsed in school and was rushed to hospital where advanced liver cancer was diagnosed. The children witnessed the ambulance arriving in school and were told by the staff what had happened.

The head teacher never returned to school and the children missed him greatly. They often asked their teachers to send him messages and pieces of their work. Staff explained to children how ill Mr Bigger was and when he died everyone involved with the children and the school gathered together in the hall where the deputy head teacher explained what had happened. The same day, parents also received a letter in which they were told about the death and how their child might respond. The head teacher's family knew he would have wanted some pupils to be at his funeral and nearly twenty attended. The day afterwards a thanksgiving was held for everyone in the school and many of the children said 'goodbye' and contributed personal messages which expressed how fond of Mr Bigger they had been.

Chapter 2

Family Bereavement

Bereavement for children is influenced by many factors including their age, level of cognitive understanding and the relationship which they had with the person who died. These factors will influence the child's emotional and behavioural responses. Separation has a powerful effect on young babies and as children grow older the effects become more complex and powerful. This not only applies to children: separation from a person who is needed for whatever reason may cause anxiety in adults too. As babies we learn that if we protest about our separation, an adult will come and comfort us. This lays the foundation for understanding that comfort is attainable through our actions and our emotional responses. Gradually young children learn to cope with separation and come to understand that changes as well as disappearances are reversible. But when life experiences prove that some losses (such as those through death) are permanent, high levels of anxiety may be attached to separation.

Bowlby (1969) outlined several prerequisites for helping children come to terms with family grief. He suggested that where they were bereaved but had experience of secure relationships prior to the death, they were more likely to achieve a healthy resolution to their loss. Bowlby defined three stages to achieve resolution of grief: firstly, children need to be given open and honest information as soon as possible after the event and to have their questions answered. Secondly they need to be active participants in the rituals surrounding death and aware of adult responses to loss. Thirdly they need a secure and sustained relationship with an adult whom they know and trust.

There is evidence (for example, Herbert 1991, Murray Parkes 1983) that working with a family is the most effective way of helping bereaved children. However most children have far less control and access to information than adults do. It is these areas of control and access which separate children's experience of death from that of the adults involved. Children adapting to grief need both cognitive and emotional understanding of what has happened. The starting point should be helping parents and primary carers to support the child in this process.

Information and feelings

Where children feel secure they will generally endeavour to get the information which is important to them by asking questions. Having obtained an answer which satisfies their curiosity for the time being, they may appear to carry on as normal. However it is not unusual for children in the early years to return to the initial question again and again until they feel that the answer they receive makes sense to them. For adults this repetition can seem very tiresome particularly if they are grieving themselves or the questions appear shocking. Perhaps the most important thing to remember is that a child's question should be answered in the spirit in which it was asked.

Telling sad things – breaking the news

The best people to break bad news are without exception the parents or adults who know the child well. Preferably the setting in which the information is given should be familiar and where possible the information should be as accurate as permits. For example, it is helpful to use the word 'dead' since euphemisms and metaphors are easily misconstrued, especially by young children who may be confused if they attempt to merge abstract and concrete concepts. If the death was expected and the child has been aware of this, then there will be a known context in which the event has happened. If not, children should be given some facts, for example, 'There has been a bad accident' or 'The sickness was just too much for... to carry on'.

Children's responses to hearing the news of death were explored in Chapter 1 but we would do well to remind ourselves that their first reactions may fluctuate from bitter weeping and anguish through to denial and protest.

How to break bad news

- Have someone the child knows break the news.
- Choose a familiar place.
- Give the information accurately, and, if possible, supported by facts about the context in which the death occurred.
- Use the words 'dead', died' etc.
- Allow uninterrupted time to sit with the child after the news has been given.
- Repeat the information.
- Allow the child to respond in any way they wish as long as they are not putting themselves at risk.
- Encourage children to ask questions.
- Reassure the child that someone will continue to care for them.

Telling children about an anticipated death

Information is essential if children are expected to cope with death realistically. Yet so often adults avoid the subject in the belief that children will cope better. This idea that 'ignorance is bliss' often leads to a concealment of the facts, especially if the death is anticipated. It may also deprive families from making the best use of the time which is left.

The effect of breaking bad news will inevitably be immediate psychological injury to the child who hears it, but as we will discover later in this section concerning life-limited and life-threatened children, young people are acutely aware of the emotional responses of adults and adept at piecing together bits of information. Children should be encouraged to ask questions since what they ask is often an indication of how they are gradually building up a picture of what is happening. Children are practical creatures who find it easier than adults to live in the present.

How can adults help?

- Prepare the child as soon as possible about what is expected to happen.
- Do not give false expectations in an attempt to alleviate the child's pain.
- Allow the child to spend time with the person.
- Avoid separation from family members where possible.
- Keep daily routines as normal as possible at home and at school.
- Encourage family members to talk together about what will happen.

Participating in rituals

Rituals are an important part of everyday life and death (Rando 1985). Through ritual people come to accept the reality of situations and to mark what has happened symbolically. Funerals provide a bridge between life and death where there is an opportunity to say 'goodbye' to the person and to bring some kind of equilibrium to what is often a chaotic situation. Funerals also allow other people to come together to support the bereaved family.

Dyregrov (1991) says 'Adults have a tendency to exclude children from the adult world when it comes to rituals'. But just like adults, children need to have the opportunity to say 'farewell' and to participate in a ceremony which will help them to make the 'unreal' become real. However, there is some anecdotal evidence to suggest that involving children in rituals without adequate preparation may lead to behavioural difficulties later on. Conversely, Weller *et al.* (1988) argue that where school children know what to expect, attendance at funerals is a positive experience.

The decision whether a child should see a person after they have died must be a family one. As we approach the millennium it is probably still the exception rather than the rule, but sometimes children express a deep desire to see the person who they love after they have died; they may become bitter and enraged if they feel they are excluded. If a child wishes to pay a visit to the dead person, preparation beforehand is essential. This should include an explanation of how the dead person will look different from when they were alive. If adults have already visited the body, they will be able to give the child more information so that the context in which the visit will take place will be known. This helps to allay fears.

One mother of a child with special educational needs explained the visit to the Chapel of Rest like this:

Saying Goodbye to Daddy

Daddy's body is safe in a special place.
It is lying in a special box called a coffin.
The coffin is on a table. It is open.
You can see Daddy's body.
Daddy looks asleep. He is very still. His eyes are closed.
Daddy cannot move or talk.
Daddy is dead.
A lady will take us to see Daddy.
The room is very quiet.
There are candles and flowers.
We can go to say 'goodbye' to Daddy.

The same mother recorded her words in symbols so that they could be used as a reminder of the event later on (Figure 2.1).

How can adults help?

- Allow the child to visit the dead person where possible.
- Prepare children carefully before the visit, explaining what to expect.
- Visit the body with a family member or someone who knows the child.
- Allow children to touch the body if they want to.
- Encourage children to express whatever emotions they wish.
- Allow time to communicate or to 'play out' impressions of the visit afterwards.

Before the funeral

Before the funeral it is also helpful if information can be given to children. This might include describing the building in which the service will take place; how the coffin will be carried into the place and where it will be put; the people who will take part in the service and what they will do.

The same family who took their young son to see his father's body explained the funeral using symbols, as in Figure 2.2:

We are going to the church.
Lots of people are going to say goodbye to Daddy.
Daddy's body is in the coffin. The lid of the coffin is shut.
There will be flowers on the coffin.
Some men will carry Daddy's body to the front of the church.
We will listen to some people talking about how special Daddy was.
We will sing some songs.
We are sad Daddy is dead.

For young children who have not developed abstract concepts, it will be helpful if they are able to participate in rituals surrounding the death, for

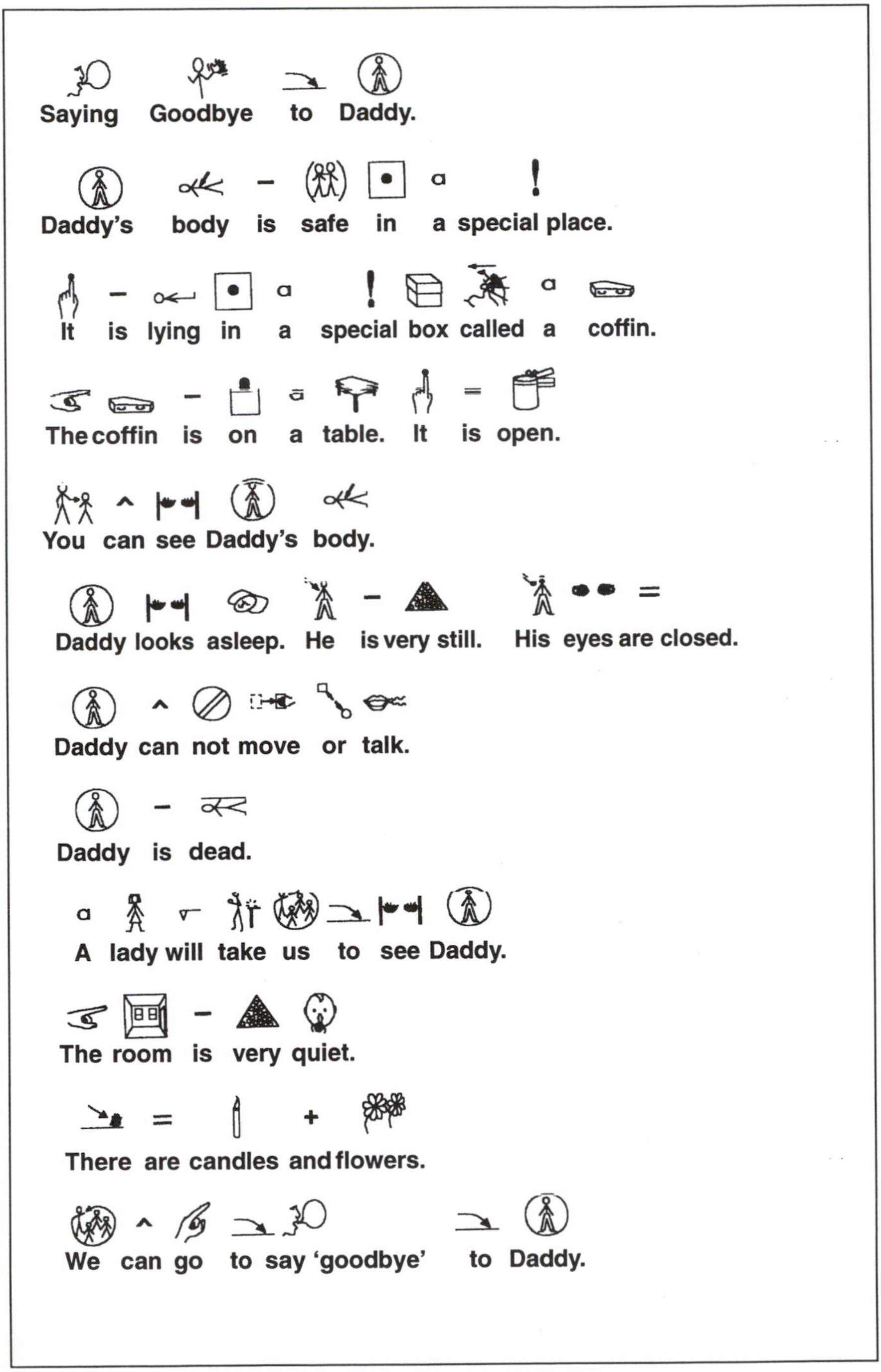

Saying   Goodbye   to   Daddy.

Daddy's   body   is   safe   in   a special place.

It   is   lying   in   a   special box called a   coffin.

The coffin   is   on   a   table.   It   is   open.

You   can   see Daddy's   body.

Daddy looks asleep.   He   is very still.   His eyes are closed.

Daddy can not move   or talk.

Daddy   is   dead.

A   lady will take us   to see Daddy.

The room   is   very quiet.

There are candles and flowers.

We   can go   to say 'goodbye'   to Daddy.

Figure 2.1 Communicating with a child with special needs

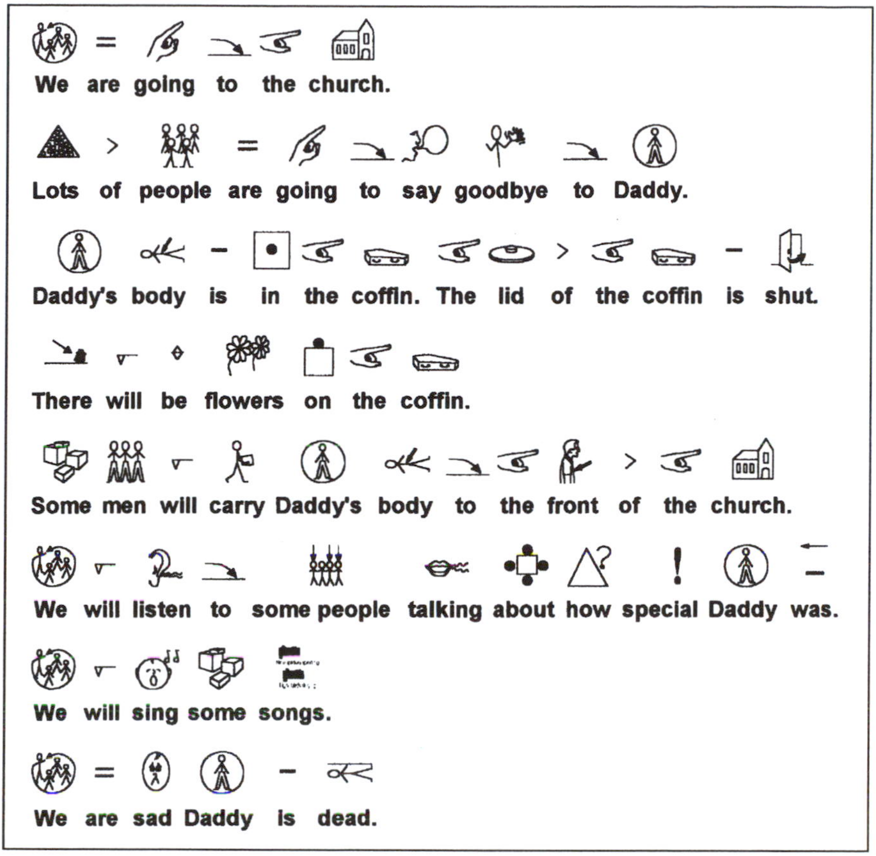

We are going to the church.

Lots of people are going to say goodbye to Daddy.

Daddy's body is in the coffin. The lid of the coffin is shut.

There will be flowers on the coffin.

Some men will carry Daddy's body to the front of the church.

We will listen to some people talking about how special Daddy was.

We will sing some songs.

We are sad Daddy is dead.

Figure 2.2 Symbols used to describe the funeral

example doing a drawing to be put in the coffin before the funeral or placing some flowers on the coffin at the funeral. Older children and adolescents should be encouraged to do what they feel is right. This may include spending some time alone with the deceased person before the funeral or taking an active role in the organisation or format of the funeral service. Other youngsters may not wish to be active participants in the rituals immediately after the death or at the funeral. As a rule of thumb, adults should respect their wishes.

If the body of the person is to be cremated it is particularly important that young children know that being dead means not being able to move, eat, breathe etc. Where children have had past experience of pets dying and have witnessed the burial of these, they may have an understanding of decay. They should be helped to understand that just as a body which is dead and decays feels no sensations, so it is during cremation. For children from faith backgrounds this may be easier since they may be familiar with the idea of a body being a 'shell' which is left behind after the spirit has gone. Figure 2.3 shows symbols to communicate:

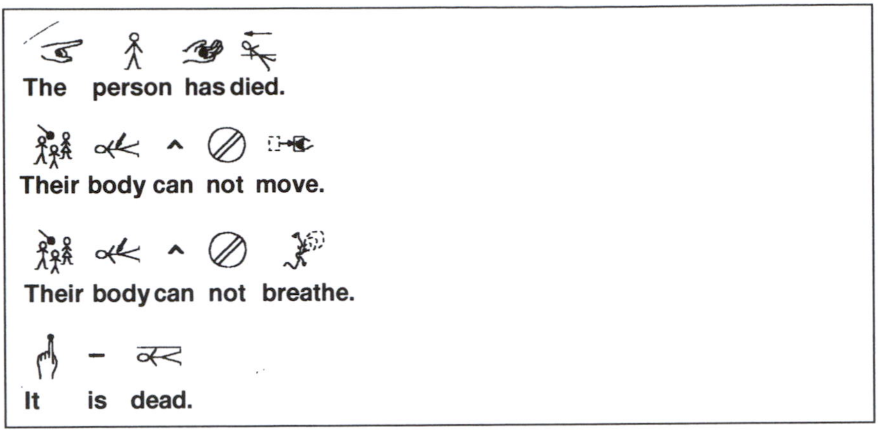

The person has died.

Their body can not move.

Their body can not breathe.

It is dead.

Figure 2.3 Symbols which can help communicate with a bereaved child

The person has died.
Their body cannot move.
Their body cannot breathe.
It is dead.

How can adults help children at funerals?
- Ensure that the child is accompanied by a parent or an adult they know.
- Encourage participation in the service if the child wishes.
- Encourage concrete expressions of grief and show children how these are important in graveyards and gardens of remembrance.
- Do not expect young children to be seated quietly for a long time during a service.
- Allow children to see the coffin buried or to attend the crematorium if they wish.

The fact that the initial shock of a death and the funeral are over will not mean children do not require ongoing support. Indeed it is often after the event that youngsters will need help in coming to terms with what has happened.

How can adults help?
- Encourage children to talk about the funeral.
- Avoid separation from family members where possible.
- Encourage children to return to the grave or the garden of remembrance if they wish to do so.
- Allow children to witness the grief experienced by adults.
- Talk about faith or cultural aspects of death which are appropriate to the child's family.
- Keep the memory of the deceased person alive.

Supportive-carers and counsellors would do well to realise the unique nature of each family's experience of a bereavement. Within the family unit every person will experience emotions which are individual to them. The experience of grief can be so overwhelming that it is hard to recognise other people's needs.

Sally was ten when her Mummy died. She did not attend the funeral and her mother's belongings were all removed to a charity shop whilst she was at school. Her father first began to realise Sally felt very alone in her grief when he noticed the family photograph albums had been opened and videos had been watched before he got home from work. For Sally these belongings were the only tangible reminders of her Mummy but she felt unable to share her grief with her father.

Children who need specialised professional support

There are occasions such as disasters when the circumstances of a death will cause a child to experience complicated grief. Intervention by highly trained personnel may help in the short term and also prevent adverse long term consequences, such as post-traumatic stress disorder. Children from dysfunctional or broken families may find little structure, support and continuity at home after a bereavement. In circumstances such as these it is imperative that any help offered is matched as closely as possible to the individual needs of the child.

Generally it is not how the child is responding to the bereavement which is significant, but for how long. After several months have elapsed the child may be experiencing clinical grief if:

- they appear sad or depressed all the time;
- they are unable to relax or have not returned to activities which interested them before the bereavement;
- they lack self-esteem or express feelings of self-recrimination or worthlessness;
- they become persistently aggressive;
- they seem withdrawn;
- they are suffering from bouts of physical illness;
- they are perpetually tired;
- they have lost weight and are not regaining it;
- they become involved with drugs, alcohol, stealing etc.;
- they pretend that nothing has happened.

How can adults help?

- Be familiar with the child's home background, including faith and culture, and share these religious and cultural beliefs with the child.
- Allow children to express their grief.

- Allow children time to fully understand and to come to terms with what has happened.
- Encourage children to ask questions and be consistent in the answers.
- Accept children's individual responses to what has happened (children are not a homogeneous group).
- Keep routines as normal as possible and encourage usual activities with peers.
- Involve children in ceremonies and rituals where possible.
- Explain the range of emotional responses associated with bereavement.
- Encourage young children to engage in play.
- Help children's peer group to understand what has happened.
- Help children to organise their memories of the person.

The death of a parent

Death is not in the scheme of things when you are a child. It is often premature and unexpected. It is an event which interferes with the normal process of growing up and plays on emotions which may never have been experienced before. In short, the death of a parent is shocking and the foundations of a child's life are rocked; their confidence in the world they know is destroyed (see Figure 2.4).

For a child whose parent has died, the bewilderment and confusion may be both in the world around and within themselves. The long-term emotional difficulties may be considerable. Brown and Harris (1989) believe that the death of a parent before the age of twelve is likely to increase the chances of depressive reactions in adulthood. However, Segal and Simkins (1996) are more positive, saying that the quality of care children receive after the death of a parent is crucial to their later well-being.

In addition to the sorrow and loneliness experienced when a parent dies, children may feel doubly abandoned by their surviving parent who is struggling to manage their own grief and may have difficulty maintaining the status quo. Anger and guilt may also be part of children's feelings if they believe that they were to blame for what happened. This is especially prevalent when there has been conflict or anger shown towards the person who has died or with young children in the magical stage of *conceptual* thinking.

Many children will deny the reality of their parent's death because quite simply, the experience and the long-term consequences are too painful to manage. Dyregrov (1991) describes this response as 'automatic emotional defence' and he writes of children who on hearing the news, turn to issues such as, 'Can I use his bed now?' or 'Can I take part in the funeral?' (p. 30).

Where children develop strategies like these it is not unusual for strong or violent feelings to emerge in other circumstances. Their reactions may then be out of proportion to the issue in hand.

Dominic was eleven when his father died. He appeared to cope with the news in a very matter-of-fact way. However, the night before the funeral, his mother asked him to clean his shoes ready for the morning. He stormed out of the kitchen in a rage declaring, 'I suppose the way I look is more important to you than just being there to say goodbye.'

Other children will be more concerned with practicalities and they ask questions like 'Where will my pocket money come from?' 'Who will look after me now?' 'Are you still going to be able to buy me those new trainers you promised me?'

Idealising the parent who has died or placing them on a pedestal is very common across the five to sixteen year age range. For some children, this response suppresses any natural feelings of anger directed at the dead person who has *left* them. Furthermore, the surviving parent may be made to feel inadequate. Other youngsters attempt to role-play their dead parent and adopt mature behaviour taking on more responsibilities than they would normally be expected to do for their age. A mutually supportive relationship between the young person and the surviving parent is arguably good, but not if it means the loss of their own childhood.

Holiday times and family occasions may be particularly painful after a parental death but it is important to maintain routines as far as possible.

Tina was fourteen the Christmas after her father was killed. On Christmas morning she stayed in bed as long as she could and then told her mother she was going for a walk. When her mother reminded her it was Christmas day she said 'I'm going out anyway because I don't see any point in sitting around pretending to be happy.' Later she returned home and cried in her mother's arms. This was the first time in the eight months after the death Tina had showed any grief.

Figure 2.4 My mummy cried when my daddy died. Sally, aged four

Complicated grief

Black and Urbanowicz (1987) and Raphael (1984), have shown that over half of a group of children studied suffered from long-term psychological problems for up to a year after the death of their parent. Two years later 30 per cent of the same young people were still experiencing adverse reactions, some of which might be described as 'pathological grief'. However it should not be extrapolated from such research that all children who experience the death of a parent are destined to suffer serious emotional problems. More work is needed into children who do well after the death of a parent.

Violent or sudden death of a parent

Bereavement is particularly hard when it is violent or sudden. The images left in children's minds may be debilitating and they may lose trust in the world (see Figure 2.5). Small children may focus their play around the trauma. Bergen (1958) writes of a child of four years who had watched one of her parents being murdered. She seized paints and a brush and, after painting the hands red, stabbed herself in the chest with the paint brush.

Where death has occurred suddenly, some children will recall events which happened immediately before, examining conversations and their own relationship with the person in great detail. Rebecca Abrams (1992) writes 'Perhaps the hardest aspect of parents' death for young people – and the one most consistently overlooked and misunderstood – is that death, mourning and grief involve feelings of helplessness and lack of control that are exceptionally difficult to cope with when you are at precisely the stage in your own life when you need to feel powerful and in control.'

Some children will need support or extra help and counselling after the death of a parent, especially if they show evidence of:

- preoccupation with death;
- changed behaviour (for example withdrawal);
- compulsive care-giving to siblings or other adults;
- euphoria or putting the deceased person on a pedestal;
- accident proneness or psychosomatic illnesses;

Figure 2.5 I have a fright in my head. Rob, aged four

• unwillingness to speak about the deceased person;
• lack of capacity to form new relationships.

What do children need?

- Routines which are as normal as possible.
- Help understanding their surviving parent's grief.
- Reassurance their own thoughts or behaviour did not cause the death.
- Opportunities to express how they feel.

How can adults help?

- Provide opportunities for children to understand what has happened and to express how they feel.
- Reassure children that although grief is painful, it is normal.
- Provide opportunities for contact with their peers for social events.
- Provide information about the circumstances of the death in language which is accessible.

The death of a sibling

When a child dies, they die at the wrong end of life, and this is something which interferes with other children's sense of security in the world. Dyregrov (1991).

The responses of siblings to children who are life-limited or life-threatened are discussed later in this book. However, it is still worth reflecting here on the powerful effects which the death of a brother or sister will have on a child. Many of the responses will mirror those which happen when a parent dies.

The impact which a child's death places on a family is profound. Surviving children have to cope with the grief and tensions which exist within themselves and within their parents. Parents often become over-protective towards surviving siblings, fearing something might happen to them. In extreme circumstances this may hinder surviving children's developing independence or conversely, the child may feel a loss of identity if they are persuaded to follow in their brother's or sister's footsteps.

Dyregrov (1991) describes what he calls potential *severe problems* for surviving siblings if they were present when their brother or sister died. He writes about children who blame themselves and who continue to live with *survivor guilt* for many years.

Ellen was nearly eight when one of her twin sisters died of a cot death (SIDS). She told me, 'It just isn't fair. She and Rachael [the surviving twin] should have grown up together. They were a pair you know. Sometimes I wish for Rachael I had been the one who forgot to breathe and died.'

If children are aware of the death of a sibling in another family, they may worry about whether the same illness or accident may happen to themselves. Against this backcloth, it is inevitable that children who experience a sibling's death will have a different view of the world. They will develop new assumptions and will need to adapt to changes in their lives.

What will siblings need?

- A home environment and routine which is as unchanged as possible.
- Reassurance they were not to blame.
- Opportunities to express their feelings in any way they choose (as long as neither their own welfare nor anyone else's is at risk).
- Parents who show their own grief.
- Information about what happened.

How can adults help?

- Keep the family together as far as possible.
- Reassure surviving siblings they were not to blame.
- Explain what happened, using language which is accessible and clearly understood.
- Give surviving siblings opportunities to express their emotions and reassurance that anything that they might feel is 'normal'.
- Share grief with children.
- Reassure siblings how much they are loved.

Suicide of a family member

Suicide creates a difficult situation for both bereaved adults and children. For a child, such deaths challenge their thoughts about what people can do and touch upon their own destructive impulses, their helplessness and dependence. Dyregrov (1991).

For children, the reality that someone can take their own life may make them feel deserted and let down. Even more distressing perhaps is the experience of the child who has discovered the body. Whatever the circumstances, those left after a suicide often experience complicated grief, especially if the death was caused through violent means such as hanging or shooting. Even young children may have fantasies about what happened, feel responsible for the event or, at worst, harbour thoughts that their own life is not worth living.

Barraclough and Hughes (1987) says not all suicide will result in complicated grieving. However, Raphael (1984) emphasises that in connection with adolescence, it may bring 'shame, stigma and guilt'. Complicated grieving, Raphael says, seems a likely outcome for many of the survivors of suicide. This is particularly so if the suicide has happened at the time when family relationships have been fraught or full of ambivalence.

Suicidal thoughts of joining the dead person are commonly experienced (Hindmarch 1993). Although these responses often seem to be unacceptable, their expression may bring some relief. Whatever the circumstances, children and adults alike will experience mixed feelings which are often very intense, volatile and difficult to bear. For children, the alternation of these feelings may be totally overwhelming. No less difficult, but seldom discussed, is the child who lives with the attempted suicide of a person close to them. For these young people there may be a deep-seated fear of a reoccurrence of what happened.

> Adrian was thirteen when his mother took an overdose after his father was found guilty of theft. When he went to see her afterwards in the hospital he could be heard shouting in the accident and emergency department, 'Promise me, swear to me, you will never, never, do this again.'

There is some empirical evidence (Valente *et al.* 1988, Raphael 1984) which suggests that teenagers who have experienced a suicide of someone close to them may be at greater risk of taking their own lives.

Dyregrov (1991) outlines several factors which should alert adults to children who may be contemplating ending their own lives.

- Preoccupation with themes of death or expressing suicidal thoughts.
- Giving away prized possessions.
- Appearance of peace, relief, contentment, especially following a period of unrest.
- Sudden and extreme changes in eating habits.
- Withdrawal from friends and family or other major behavioural changes, such as aggression.
- Changes in sleeping patterns.
- Changes in school performance.

Barraclough and Hughes (1987) write about the consequences of bereavement through suicide for surviving relatives: 'The shock of the event, the trauma of the police enquiry and the inquest, gossip and disapproval amongst friends and neighbours, publicity in the local newspaper and sometimes radio and television, all add to the relatives' short term distress.' (p. 134).

Because suicide is viewed by much of society as unacceptable and there is a stigma attached to it, families often feel unworthy or unable to ask for help. For many families, when a member commits suicide there are major problems left behind for the survivors. Not least, partners and children may feel confused about the relationship which they had with the deceased person. Why didn't they give any warning of what they were about to do? Or, if warning and threats were given, why were they disbelieved or ignored?

Throughout the book we will discover that adults are often reluctant to share open and honest information with children. This is especially so when death occurs through suicide and children are given inadequate, incorrect explanations or told half truths.

Perhaps the most commonly asked question after suicide is 'Why?' and children will either pose this themselves or be surrounded by other people who do. Young people cannot live their lives in a vacuum where they are protected from situations which are difficult to handle. Telling children facts which they will be able to grasp will in some ways equip them to face other people and prevent them from denying what happened. It may also stop them being at risk of developing serious psychiatric problems.

How can adults help?
- Acknowledge the shock of what has happened.
- Reassure children they were not to blame.
- Reassure children life is worth living.
- Give children as much time as they need to adjust to life without the person who is no longer there.
- Allow children to feel angry.
- Allow children to talk about suicide and how they feel.

Figure 2.6 When you die you goes in a black van. It is a ride in a box. Pippa, aged five

Chapter 3

Life-limited and Life-threatened Children

In Great Britain approximately 15,000 children and young people under the age of 20 die each year. The serious illness or death of a child is a disturbing and shocking event. Judd (1989) refers to it as 'out of season'. Although Black (1989) writes of the remoteness of childhood death in the twentieth century, for some children and their families it will remain a stark reality.

Children who die contradict all expectations, yet in Victorian times, parents saw about a quarter to a third of their children die before they reached ten years of age (Stannard 1997). Today medical science plays an important role in sustaining life. Indeed, over 80 per cent of babies born of only one kilo birth weight will survive. Where tragedy occurs it is often because of injury, congenital abnormality, cancer, cardiovascular disease or AIDS.

The context of childhood death and children's experience of mortality has changed. In the past, most deaths occurred at home and death and illness was witnessed first-hand with children caring for the sick and present at the time of death and the funeral. The ancient nursery rhyme 'Ring-a-ring o' roses' bears witness to a game played by children during the Great Plague and Black Death of the fourteenth century. The 'rosie-ring' refers to swelling lymph nodes and 'a pocket-full of posies' to an amulet as a protection from the disease. 'Achoo' describes the flu-like symptoms associated with the plague and 'all fall down' refers to the inevitable death of the victims. In the twenty-first century most people will die in hospitals or in institutions and death will not be within children's everyday experience.

Life-threatening illness plunges children into a confusing and previously unknown world, where people speak in medical jargon, they are subjected to painful treatment and uncertainty. Normal routines are shattered and relationships are turned upside-down. In short, the definition of life-threatening illness as 'a condition which endangers life or has significant risk of death' Doka (1993), falls short of describing what happens to a child and their family. Doka is however very helpful in describing the phases of life-threatening illness.

Phase 1: pre-diagnosis

This period prior to diagnosis is often one when the seriousness of the condition is suspected.

Phase 2: diagnostic

During this phase the illness is named and the reality of possible death is faced for the first time. It is a time of exceeding stress for families who often say that they experience a *first death* at the time of diagnosis.

Phase 3: chronic

This phase is generally marked by extensive medical treatment and often physical changes in the child. Families commonly deny the severity of the disease as they struggle to keep life as normal as possible. It is a time when parents need to begin to grieve the loss of normality in their lives.

Phase 4: terminal

The illness has now progressed so that the inevitable outcome is death. Treatment is directed at pain relief and aggressive intervention in order to maintain life is abandoned. Some researchers have attempted to describe task-based models to describe adults' responses to each phase. These will be discussed later in the chapter.

Children's understanding of life-threatening illness

Some researchers (Judd 1989) conclude that although children may not have reached a conceptual understanding of death, most are aware that something is physically wrong with their body. Vernick (1973) claims that weakness may often be interpreted as acceptance of death by the child but this is vehemently challenged by Kubler-Ross (1983), who writes of children's determination to survive against all the odds.

Most researchers and medical practitioners support the philosophy that even when faced with ultimate death, it is important to maintain in children a sense of hope, not only for themselves, but also for those who love and care for them (Judd 1989, Spinetta 1975). Adult theories which suggest that if children are unaware of the seriousness of their illness they will not be frightened, are refuted by those who work with life-threatened children (Brown 1994, Waechter 1971). Children in hospitals or hospices where other young people are dying or who have died, seem to show an enhanced awareness of death (and in some cases increased anxiety). Brown (1993) tells of children with AIDS and HIV on a paediatric ward of a hospital who were aware of memorial services and were angry that the adults who surrounded them were able to live normal lives outside the hospital. Amongst another group of youngsters on the oncology ward of the same hospital was a child who had heard words such as 'kill' and 'invade' in relation to the therapy given to treat her disease. Understandably she had fantasies about warfare and was constantly checking she was not being attacked.

Bluebond-Langner (1995) says children who are life-limited or life-threatened have a more mature understanding of death than their healthy peers.

This process involves encounters with illness that are paralleled by changes in their self-perception. First the child understands they are seriously ill and gradually moves towards a realisation of acute, chronic and fatal sickness. It is important to recognise however that these phases are not clear-cut stages. They may overlap and in some cases be delayed by a pathological grief (Herbert 1996).

Diagnosis	1	2	3	4	5
	My illness is serious	I am taking powerful drugs and they have side effects	I know why I am having the treatment	I am suffering relapses and remissions	The pattern of relapses and remissions will end in death

(based on Herbert 1996)

Stage 1 is dependent on observing how other people respond and hearing what they say. After receiving treatment and visiting hospitals/clinics the child reaches Stage 2 which often includes a remission in the illness. After the first relapse, Stage 3 is reached and as a result of several more relapses and remissions the child realises at Stage 4 this is the pattern in their life. When the child realises that someone else has died they parallel their own experience and Stage 5 is achieved.

Whether a child should be told of the seriousness of their illness is open to debate. Kubler-Ross (1983) says, 'Although all patients have the right to

Figure 3.1 Donna, aged 12, told the nurses her parents made her angry when they withheld information from her

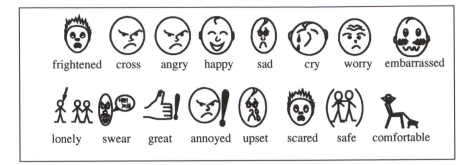

Figure 3.2 Symbols which communicate feelings

know, not all patients have the need to know'. Generally it is believed parents' wishes should be respected regarding how much, if any, information should be given to the child. Herbert (1996) believes:

- Parents are important as role models in determining a child's response to their illness or death.
- Where parents are able to break the news calmly, the child will cope better.
- Many children are resilient to stress and they may cope better than their parents.
- Children need to know the truth.

Children who are aware they are having information withheld from them may feel alone, deceived and vulnerable (see Figure 3.1). Often they are battling with fantasies about death. How information is conveyed to the child is important. It needs to be done in an age-appropriate and cognitive-appropriate level. Figure 3.2 shows symbols used by children with profound and multiple learning difficulties. The greatest support to the child is his or her family, but peer group support is also vital.

Children may communicate their awareness of the severity of their illness verbally or through play, writing, drawing or the arts. Kubler-Ross (1983) describes these responses as 'pre-conscious awareness' from the 'inner-spiritual, intuitive quadrant' (p. 134). Doka (1993) advises that adults should consider how they will give information to children, a view supported by Easson (1970) who writes: 'the best treatment of the dying youngster can be based only on the knowledge of what his approaching death means to him and how the young patient can reasonably cope with this very personal reality.' (p. 5). Figure 3.3 reveals a child's knowledge of her approaching death.

The psychological effects of children facing a life-threatening illness are dependent on many factors including the child's age, the seriousness of the illness, the degree to which normal activities can be performed and how body image is affected. Parkes (1972a) describes children's reactions as being very like those of adults who are bereaved and suffering grief. Responses include initial shock or numbness on learning the news; denial of the seriousness of the illness; anger about the restrictions the disease imposes on their life; a sense of injustice;

Figure 3.3 When I die I will be an angel. Poppy, aged four and a half

depression, sadness and helplessness associated with being out of control as the illness progresses; bargaining, in an attempt to postpone the inevitable outcome; and finally, acceptance that death will happen. Serious illness during adolescence may cause particularly turbulent emotions. Just as young people are achieving independence and separation from their families, they are cheated by serious health problems and by reminders that their goal of adulthood will never be fulfilled.

Children's questions about their illness will often catch adults off their guard. However they usually phrase questions in a way which lets adults know how much information they require. Therefore, it is very important to listen carefully to what children ask and to observe how they are responding. If they do not understand, it is likely they will return to the question again. But it is not always easy to judge exactly what a child is asking. Reflecting a question back or re-phrasing it in a way which encourages the child to give more information about their underlying concerns can be very helpful. For example, the child who asks 'Will I have a pain when I die?', may have a deep-seated fear of his or her own capacity to cope. The adult who asks, 'Why do you think you might have a pain?' will help him or her to express their anxiety and will often be able to offer the child reassurance. Children who have been ill for a long time may be very aware of what is happening to them, through conversations they have heard or observations they have made about the behaviour of the adults around them. Figure 3.4 illustrates this awareness.

Communicating with children who are facing the end of life

It is a challenging task for those who have to break the news to someone that their life is threatened. Telling a child must be amongst the most difficult and painful things anyone will ever have to do. Throughout this book I make a plea for open and honest communication between families facing death and those who care for them.

The philosophy and belief of the family

It is vital that the family's views and experience concerning life and death are taken into account. This will include:

- how family members express their grief;
- the past history of the family concerning loss and change;
- religious or cultural perspectives of the family concerning what happens at death and beyond.

The child's age, experience and developmental level, including their concept of death

How children are likely to respond to the news of their own life-limitation will determine the way in which they are told the news. It should include:

- helping children to express their fears and concerns;
- helping children to communicate what they know about their illness;
- helping children to express their own preferences and needs.

Figure 3.4 My people at home are frightened. Thomas, aged three

How the family is likely to cope

The strategies which families adopt for dealing with any crisis will generally be an indicator of how they will cope with a life-threatening illness. Families need not only to witness how their child is cared for, but to experience how their own emotional, psychological and spiritual needs are met. They may be helped by:

- giving them opportunities to reflect on how they have coped with past experiences of crisis;
- giving individuals within the family opportunities to reflect on personal coping strategies;
- giving families opportunities to recognise the unique way in which each individual copes in the face of adversity.

Children are acutely aware of how messages are conveyed and how news is given. Despite advances in medical science children still die. They are often removed from familiar surroundings and nursed by people who do not know them and give them medication which may be unpleasant or lead to side effects. Paediatric pain control is improving (Duffy 1997) but young children and those with special needs may not possess skills to communicate their level of distress. Some children with special educational needs in a hospice school room have found the symbols designed by Widget Software UK helpful (Figure 3.2).

Meeting individual needs of children

In working with life-threatened children I have frequently asked the following questions: What does the child want to know? What does the child need to know? What can the child understand?

Taking into account children's developmental understanding, these questions might be translated:

Babies, and toddlers' needs

- Help coping with pain.
- Frequent physical contact (or touching) from the primary carers.
- Frequent contact with the voices of the primary carers.
- Normal routines as far as possible.
- Opportunities to play and to interact with family members.

Pre-school

- Reassurance that any separation from primary carers is unavoidable.
- Reassurance that the illness is not a form of punishment.
- Open communication in easily understood language.
- Explanations about medical procedures.

• Constant reassurance about love and care from their family.
• Access to communication which will help indicate levels of pain or distress.
• Routines which are as normal as possible.
• Opportunities to interact with peers and family members where possible.
• Opportunities to communicate fears and concerns.

Figure 3.5 is a drawing by a child in this age group.

5–7 years

• Open and honest communication about the nature of the illness.
• Opportunities to communicate preferences, needs, fears and concerns.
• Maintenance of familiar routines as far as possible.
• Constant reassurance of the love and care of family members, peers and friends.
• Access to communication which will help them articulate levels of pain or anxiety.
• Access to educational activities and hobbies.
• Liaison with school.

7–9 years

• Open and honest communication about the nature and inevitable outcome of their illness.
• Opportunities to express their own opinions, wishes, anxieties.
• Constant reassurance of the love and care of key people in their lives.
• Freedom to make decisions about their own pain control and care.
• Opportunities to express their awareness of how family members are responding.
• Maintenance of familiar cultural or religious traditions.

Figure 3.5 My mummy will be an angel too. She will come to heaven and look after me. Mary, aged four

Adolescence

- Opportunities to express fears and concerns for self and family members.
- Privacy, especially when undergoing personal care.
- Opportunities to maintain autonomy and independence for as long as possible.
- Support from peer groups as well as family members.
- Involvement in decisions regarding their care.
- Maintenance of familiar cultural and religious traditions.

Figure 3.6 shows the religious background of 12 year old Grant.

How children communicate an awareness that they are dying

Whilst all children who are dying show an awareness of what is happening to them before the event happens, the acquisition and assimilation of the knowledge is a prolonged process. Where children are told that they are dying before death is imminent, Bluebond-Langner (1995) refers to the process as one of *internalisation*. Figure 3.7 shows Charlotte's understanding that she will die and what will happen afterwards. Where they are not told directly but learn what is happening, the same author refers to this as a process of *discovery*.

As children progress through the stages of their illness, their view of themselves changes as they accumulate more information. It is a process which is dependent on experience rather than on age. I met a little boy of five years old when I was working at the hospital school. He was dying of AIDS.

Figure 3.6 It will be OK. I know what will happen. Grant, aged 12

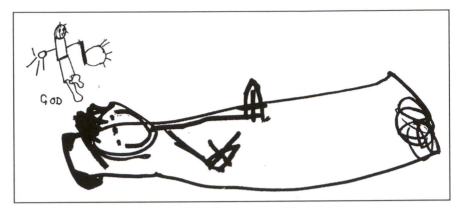

Figure 3.7 When I die God will look after me. Charlotte, aged six

An older child in the cubicle next to him had suddenly died of the same illness immediately after eating his lunch. Jason called me to his bed and told me 'I am not eating them chips and peas. He's just gone and died. If I eat this, I'll die too.'

However, another child on the ward who heard about the death did not consider her disease (brain tumour with secondary malignancy of the liver) to be as threatening. She remarked: 'He had AIDS you know – it's a very bad illness. You can't cure AIDS. People get cured of cancer.'

Interestingly, neither child had been told directly about their illness. They had learned about it through a process of discovery but they had not previously communicated any knowledge of their prognosis to either their families or to the nursing staff. The death of another child had caused them to reflect on their own condition. Figure 3.8 shows how an eleven year old girl communicated what she thought would happen after she died.

Other children in the hospital did not reveal an understanding of their illness in such and open and forthright way. Their remarks were made in passing and often to play therapists or in the school room whilst they were engaged in activities. A fourteen year old who was wheeled into the classroom daily to work on maths and English, frequently muttered under his breath 'I'm doing this for what? – there ain't no reason, ain't no use.' Another younger child made a coffin-shaped structure out of Lego and, placing a small figure from the Playmobil hospital into the coffin said, 'Go in there now – they'll put you in there and after five days they'll take you downstairs to the chapel and sing "The Wheels on the Bus Go Round and Round."' She then turned and said, 'I don't want that song – that's a baby's song. I don't want to go downstairs. I don't want a song. Tell them (the nurses) I don't want that song.' These youngsters implied their death, but they did not acknowledge it openly.

As children's illness progresses they often refer less to treatment and more to how the time which they have left will be spent. Certainly the children known to me who were terminally ill had an urgent need to achieve ambitions. They pleaded to be taken outside the hospital for social events even though

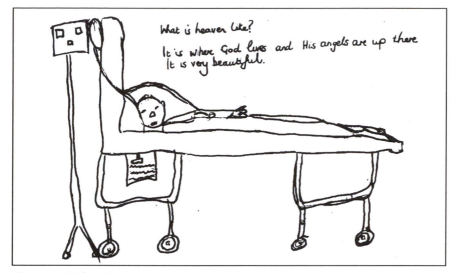

Figure 3.8 Cheryl, Year 5, communicating her thoughts

they were too ill to fully participate in their chosen activity. One lad regularly challenged me as I prepared to leave the ward with the words 'It's OK for you, you can go home.' The boy concerned had no home other than the ward to go to, but it did not prevent him from either regularly trying to 'escape' in the lift or confronting me with his words as the door closed.

Challenges like these seemed to monopolise many of the conversations I had with children. Had they been children in mainstream education their personal profiles would probably have referred to 'emotional and behavioural difficulties'. They seem to be intent on what Bluebond-Langner (1995) calls *disengaging people* in a rehearsal for the final separation of death. What is strikingly evident in these children's stories is how their understanding and response to death is related to their experience, rather than their chronological age.

Brothers and sisters who are dying

We often refer to the dying child as 'the victim of chronic or terminal illness'. But brothers, sisters and indeed entire families are partners in the same destiny. In other words, the desolation spreads far beyond the child who is affected. Bluebond-Langner (1995) describes siblings as living in 'houses of chronic sorrow'. Many siblings experience a change of role in the family and a change in status. In some families well siblings are care-takers of ill siblings or, in extreme cases, they are so effected by their family situation that they become what Almond *et al.* (1979) call *non-persons* because their parents' attention is elsewhere. As a result they may feel unsupported, neglected and confused about who they are and who they are supposed to be. Emma told me:

> Everywhere I go they call me Jason's sister. At school, at Brownies and even the people I am meant to call Aunty Mary and Uncle John next door. I am not Jason's sister. I am me. But nobody notices any more.

Well siblings often have to adjust to living away from home so that they can be cared for whilst their parents are with their brother or sister. They feel vulnerable, confused and even neglected because the stability and attention to which they have become accustomed is under threat. Rob, aged nine, said:

> I can't have my friends for my birthday in case one of them has chicken pox or a cold and he gives his germs to my sister. Because if she gets more ill she could die quicker. It's not fair. I will not get my birthday again.

Often information is confused or lacking and gleaned from overheard conversations which may have been laden with medical jargon. But this is not always the case. Jennifer's younger brother was born with cystic fibrosis and she recalls:

> In the beginning it was OK. My mum and dad had to do lots of physiotherapy. We were like a 'normal' family. Then he got older and bigger and we had to have special equipment and even an extension built onto the house. Once the builders had gone, my parents moved into the other bedroom to be near him and I hardly ever saw him after that apart from at his meal times. We never ate together as a family because someone always had to be with him in case he needed oxygen. At the end it was awful. I just wanted it to be a bit awful like it was at first.

Knowing what siblings are feeling may be very hard. Often their responses when they are first told, or at the time of death, are very revealing. Tommy aged ten, on being told his teenage sister would never come home again because she was dying of bone cancer, said 'Good, now I will be able to spend as long as I want in the bathroom.' Likewise, Nabil's response to his baby sister's cot death was 'I never wanted a sister anyway. Her bedroom was all pink and girly.'

These siblings are angry, jealous and bored with waiting for the expected tragedy to happen, but they are also expressing confusion, pain and loss in the only way that they know.

Well children often come to learn about death and dying through their interactions with their dying brother or sister. As illness progresses parents understandably devote more of their attention to the dying child and they feel ill equipped and physically and emotionally drained coping with other family members. Well children may worry about their own future. Bluebond-Langner (1989) writes, 'the signs of sorrow, illness and death are everywhere, whether or not they are spoken of. The signs are written on parents' faces.' (p. 9).

Most studies of siblings have been retrospective, but the work of Spinetta (1984) and Saurkes (1987) makes a plea for the needs of brothers and sisters of seriously and terminally ill children to be taken into account before the terminal phase. Both research studies cite evidence that siblings suffer more than patients in terms of unattended emotional needs.

Martinson *et al.* (1990) describe the effects as:

- *Loneliness, alienation and confusion* as a result of disruption in family relationships.
- *Concern* for their own health and that of family members.
- *Anger, resentment, powerlessness, rivalry*, directed at the ill child who is the focus of attention.

The younger siblings are, the more likely they are thought to be at risk, since any change in family routines may be perceived as parental rejection. Older siblings may shoulder adult responsibilities.

Jess, aged seven, said:

My mum used to read me stories at night when I went to bed, but she doesn't any more. She's too tired so she tucks me up and lets me keep the light on so I can look at books, but it's not the same.

Experiences like these exist because of the emotional and physical demands made on the parents. Siblings do not, however, describe these experiences from the time of diagnosis through to the terminal phase of the illness. It is striking how in many families life remains very much as it always was. But with normal feelings of hostility, rivalry and jealousy, between brothers and sisters, the effect of having a family member dying places a huge strain on relationships.

The responses of siblings when they are told of the death of a brother or sister are very revealing. Often they are of relief, mingled with pain, loss and loneliness and, ironically, ambivalence. Khadijah, aged 17, remarked 'Well at least it wasn't me – what a waste if all my GCSEs had been for nothing.' Then she begged me not to tell her aunt and uncle (with whom she was living) what she had said, because, as she put it, 'I know it's unfair but my family have cut me off since he got ill.'

What happens at the time of death and what brothers and sisters are told is critically important. Whatever the age of siblings, they will notice stress on adults in the family. Although the inclinations of parents to protect their children from witnessing their own grief is understandable, it is important that expressions of sadness are shown, in order that other family members may know how much they were valued and how much they will be missed.

Children lose an ally if a sibling dies. This is particularly significant if the family structure now means that they are an only child. Older siblings may feel they did not care sufficiently for their younger brother or sister. Conversely, younger ones may feel that they may never reach adulthood either. Hindmarch (1993) summarises common anxieties:

- Will I die too?
- Was I to blame?
- Who cares for me now?

How siblings grieve

The way in which siblings grieve is influenced by the manner in which the child died and also the relationship which existed prior to death. The relationship will be determined by a number of factors including birth order. The normal rivalry amongst siblings may lead to feelings of guilt after a brother or sister dies. Intense grief reaction is more common when the relationship was either very close or very negative or distant.

Virginia, aged six, told me after her elder brother had died:

> When he had his friends around and they went to his room, especially if it was a girlfriend, I wasn't allowed in there and I used to feel really cross about that. Now I wish he would come back so that I could tell him I only felt like that because I wanted to join in the grown-up things he did.

Some children may hide their grief in an attempt to shield their family. When seven year old Michael died of a brain tumour his sister Susan, aged ten, hid in a locked bedroom for nearly a week, stealing down to the kitchen for food at night and taking it back to her room. Once or twice her parents saw her briefly on the landing on the way to the bathroom but she refused to talk to them. Months later she told her teacher she had tried to 'keep her hurt inside of her'.

Raphael (1984) summarises the grief of siblings:

> In losing a sibling the child loses a playmate, a companion, someone who is a buffer against parents, someone who may love and comfort him, someone with whom he identifies and whom he admires. In short, he loses someone dearly loved as well as perhaps envied and rivalously hated.

Supporting the siblings of dying children

Children's needs are sometimes overlooked by adults who are locked in their own grief. Because of the importance of emotional bonding and attachments, the death of a sibling may have a very profound effect on surviving children. How they respond will largely depend on what they understand about death and what they have been taught and experienced in their family. Almost all children will need help during the first two years after a death to:

- understand their parents' grief;
- communicate what they are feeling;
- express their sadness and longing, especially at family times such as celebrations, birthdays and holidays.

There is a considerable body of evidence which suggests that psychiatric disorder is significantly more common in people who have been bereaved both in childhood and in adult life (Black 1993). In Lansdown and Goldman's (1988) study of 28 children whose brothers or sisters had died, the majority were found to have behavioural and emotional difficulties and low self-esteem.

Most siblings will welcome involvement in their brother or sister's care. However, like their parents, they may be reluctant or have little opportunity to communicate their confusion and anxiety. Hospitals, hospices and support services are responding by providing group meetings to provide opportunities for peers to meet together.

What do siblings need?
• The family kept together where possible.
• Information about what is happening.
• Reassurance that they were not to blame.
• Explanations using language which is accessible and clearly understood.
• Opportunities to express emotions and reassurance that their feelings are *normal*.
• Adults who will be brave enough to share their grief.
• Reassurance of their value and how much they are loved.

The extended family – grandparents

All members of families are deeply effected when a child is life-threatened. There are, however, few research studies which have explored the feelings of family members other than parents and siblings (Seligman and Darling 1989, Meyer 1993). Relatives and friends of some of the dying children I have described have communicated very powerfully a sense of unfairness and injustice. Older people have spoken of how they had an 'investment in the future' through their grandchildren. There were also references to the impact which the burden and grief experienced by the children's parents had had on them. One grandmother said:

> I know she is my grandchild but Melanie [the child's mother] is my daughter. As her mum I want so much to take away the pain like I did when she was a little girl. But I can't and that is one of the hardest things.

Grandparents also spoke of the shock they had experienced when they received the news of the diagnosis second hand. Grandmothers had usually received the news, often by phone. Grandfathers subsequently heard from their partners and, in many cases, they felt the impact of the shock rendered them at a complete loss of what to say or do. However, there were others who felt able to give emotional and practical support to their own children and grandchildren.

Interestingly, some grandparents had a much greater awareness of the impact of the sibling's illness on brothers and sisters than the parents did. Frequently family members confided in them because they felt unable to share their fears and anxieties with people in more direct contact with the dying child. The exception to the rule in the small number of families I have studied, were those where a baby was either still-born or died very soon after birth. Here maternal grandmothers and grandfathers of the baby seemed to lose communication with their daughter. Mostly their own grief appeared to make them unable to say anything and often they spoke of not wanting to intrude. In four families none of the grandparents saw the baby at all and one grandfather said:

> It's been like a bad dream. You look forward to seeing your own children grow up and become parents – you have plans for them and then it's ended before it's begun and all our son and his wife were left with was an empty crib and empty arms.

When a child is terminally ill, parents enter into a nightmare world where the terrain is uncharted, the immediate future is unpredictable and their parenting skills are challenged. Accepting that a child is dying is the hardest thing any parent can do. Denial, and resisting the inevitability of death, is natural and very common and the skills of people supporting parents are vital in helping them to acknowledge what is going to happen. However, it is not a process which should be rushed. Families need time and plenty of opportunity to share their concerns. They may feel torn between choosing aggressive treatment for a child or withdrawing therapy and thus acknowledging that no more can be done. Seldom will they be able to communicate their feelings coherently to professionals or to their family, including the child who is life-limited.

Black (1993) says:

> there is much evidence that if we do not grieve at the time we are likely to be affected throughout our lives in all kinds of subtle ways...Adults who fail to mourn are likely to deal with the issues of loss, even minor loss, in maladaptive ways.

The way in which the diagnosis stage of a child's illness is handled clearly influences how parents respond when they are faced with the news of a terminal prognosis. Amongst the case studies I have described in the paediatric hospital ward, 40 per cent of the parents had a complaint about health professionals at this stage. The most common grievance was the way in which they were told and the lack of time available to discuss the consequences for either their child or the family. A larger number (55 per cent) were critical of their GP and the time lapse before the initial referral of the child to a consultant. These delays caused parents to feel angry and reluctant to trust medical people in the future. However, there were others who bore the brunt of blame themselves for not noticing their child was ill sooner.

There are several phases which most parents who are caring for a dying child will experience:

- **numbness** on hearing the news of the child's prognosis. This may be accompanied by feelings of shock, disbelief and denial;
- **yearning** for the normality of life before the news was heard which may be accompanied by acute feelings of searching, crying, reminiscing, anger and guilt;
- **hopelessness and despair** which may be accompanied by feelings of loneliness, helplessness, depression and anxiety.

Supporting the whole family

The Royal College of Nursing defines the family as 'the child's primary support group in his or her life'. Most support services are committed to the care of the whole family and not just the patient. Almond *et al.* (1979) speak of the family as the patient.

Family communication patterns appear to be critical in determining how well families cope with illness, since the most valuable sources of support are imbedded in their relationships, open-parenting styles, and philosophy. Evidence from a number of studies suggests the family's cultural, social and educational background also influences how they cope. Furthermore the findings of Phillimore *et al.* (1994) show that economic status in families may be a factor in coping with bereavement.

Culling (1988) suggests that families who are collectively able to communicate their feelings, facilitate adaptation to life-threatening and terminal illness. Children look to their family for support especially when situations are unknown and unexpected. Typically they mirror the coping strategies shown by their parents (Moody and Moody 1991). Stephenson (1985) contrasts closed and open family communication systems which operate in the face of death. Rigidity and tightly defined roles together with strict thought and behaviour patterns characterise closed family systems. Generally the significance and impact of death is not openly acknowledged or discussed and family members may be isolated. Conversely the open family system functions in what Stephenson calls a 'nurturing' environment where the impact of death is openly recognised and adults express their thoughts and feelings, encouraging children to do likewise. He describes this as 'parents and children facilitating each other's grieving' (p. 185).

Within each of the phases of illness experienced by the child, the family will also have to develop strategies for adjusting and coping. These will differ from the diagnostic phase to the terminal phase but they may include:

- recognising the symptoms, pain and physical changes;
- adjusting to medical intervention and institutional treatment;
- developing strategies to manage stress;

- communicating effectively with professional people and carers;
- preparing for death and saying 'goodbye';
- maintaining the family identity;
- preserving relationships with partners and friends;
- expressing emotions and fears;
- accepting the finality of death.

After the death of a child

Parents may experience outrage, despair and lack of purpose at the prospect of living beyond their child. Judd (1989) quotes Frances Dominica, 'Almost without exception we have found that families fare worse in the second year than they do in the first. Into the third year many families have found a different way of living, accepting the fact that the child has died and that they have got to make some sort of life.'

Frances Dominica goes on to say that 90 per cent of what a bereaved person needs is a fellow human being to be alongside them. Bereaved parents often find keeping in touch with similar parents helpful because for many there is a sense of social isolation.

What do families need?
- Adequate and accessible information at each stage of their child's illness, given in a variety of ways.
- Professional people who will support and encourage them.
- Practical support and resources to alleviate financial burdens etc.
- People who will develop or maintain their self-esteem, helping them to feel in control.
- Opportunities to develop and sustain relationships and communications within the family and particularly with the child who is dying.
- Caring for the child in a familiar environment wherever possible.
- Opportunities to develop caring strategies allowing them to determine options and helping them to feel in control.

Chapter 4

Grief and Disability

The challenges that parents of disabled children face should not be underestimated, but we must also familiarise ourselves with the work of scholars such as Challela (1981) who claims that any birth is a crisis experience in which many parents find themselves with no previous experience or expertise. In other words as Murgatroyd and Woolfe (1993) write, 'the birth of a child usually represents an important transitional event for a family, with a relationship and structure not being the same again'. (p. 86). Caplan (1968) believes that birth creates an upset in the everyday equilibrium of life. Whilst many parents would challenge Caplan's notion of birth as a crisis, for parents of disabled children, the trauma of the event is undeniable.

The loss of a long awaited 'normal' baby represents the death of parents' ideal of what a child was to be and hand in hand with this experience is an emotional response of grief. Coupled with what Beckman and Beckman-Boyes (1993) describe as frightening and confusing information, families face a huge challenge.

Parents in crisis

One of the first dilemmas of having a child with special educational needs or some kind of disability is the shattering experience of how to cope with something which was unexpected and how to accept as a parent what is unacceptable.

It seems to me that there are some fundamental differences between the crisis of parents who have a child with a disability and human experiences of other crises. Firstly, as Murgatroyd and Woolfe (1993) suggest, parents facing disability have an objective element – the child with the disability. Generally it will be possible to examine the degree of the disability against some standard and to consider the implications of the disability for both the child and the adults. Secondly, unless a child is terminally ill or life-threatened, the disability will persist during the lifetime of the parents. Therefore, the grief which parents endure is long-term and has both physical and emotional consequences. Psychologically parents have to face the dilemma of having brought into the world something which they had not expected. They have lost their 'ideal' of a baby in which they had invested their hopes for the future.

Several authors write about the isolation which parents face as they struggle to come to terms with their shock (Hornby 1994, Hewett *et al.* 1970). Furthermore, the task of coping is a process in which parents find themselves constantly adjusting to the new demands which their growing child makes. Murgatroyd and Woolfe (1993) refer to this process as 'recurrent crises'.

In addition to psychological and physical implications, parents of children with disabilities often experience extra financial burdens as they endeavour to sustain the quality of life for their child in physical, emotional and educational terms. These tasks of psychological, social and physical coping are not mastered overnight. Neither can other people act as sole advocates for parents – they have to be enabled to act as advocates for themselves.

Grieving parents

Most parents who give birth to a child with a disability will experience grief and a period of adaptation or adjustment. Feelings of overwhelming loss combined with disbelief and anger are common, together with searching for a 'better diagnosis' in which they can invest some hope for the future. This process represents a classic model of grief.

However, parents of disabled children are often plunged into grief at each milestone and transition point in their child's life when there is no alternative but to reflect on what 'might have been'. Some researchers (Olshansky 1962, Darling 1993) have described these experiences as those of 'chronic sorrow'.

Mothers and fathers

Research has provided some interesting insights into the pace at which mothers and fathers adapt to their child born with a disability. Studies reveal that the primary carer in most families with a disabled child is the mother (Fewell and Meyer 1986, Parkes 1983, Chodorow 1990). Not surprisingly these mothers are likely to exhibit higher levels of stress than the mothers of non-disabled children (Minnes 1988, Campion 1991). Additionally, mothers take responsibility for the majority of domestic tasks in families where there is a disabled member (Barnett and Boyce 1995).

Hautamäki (1997) has suggested that very soon after a mother has given birth to a disabled child she directs all her energy into providing care for her baby. This may be in an attempt to restore her damaged self-image as a mother as she adjusts to new demands. However, the same author argues that in reality most mothers require a time of reflection or 'retesting' before becoming completely devoted to their baby. This gives them opportunities to recover interest in themselves without a conflict between their own needs and those of their child.

Carpenter and Herbert (1994) describe fathers' perceptions of themselves as 'the peripheral parent' and McConkey (1994) speaks of the 'hard to reach parent'. Research by Brotherson *et al.* (1986) and Meyer and Vadasy (1986) reveals a high incidence of emotional and psychological problems in fathers of disabled children compared with those who are parents of non-disabled children. However, the work of Hornby (1994, 1995) has found little evidence to support this theory although Lamb and Layzell (1993) suggest that less contact with the baby may lead fathers to deny the impact and extent of their child's disability.

The crucial time for fathers adjusting to being a parent of a disabled child seems to be at the moment of diagnosis, with particular reference to the way in which the news is broken and the setting in which this takes place. Not surprisingly there are parallels here with responses to shocking news in other contexts (Dyregrov 1991, Herbert 1996, Parkes *et al.* 1996).

Several programmes have been designed to support fathers (Meyer and Vadasy 1986, May 1991) and the positive effects have included diminished stress levels (Bray 1997).

Alistair, father of Stuart, now in his thirties, said:

> At first we thought there had been a mistake. Then we kept asking ourselves whether it was our fault. In the end you realise you cannot go through life burying your head in the sand. Reality of that first shock has been renewed so many times as our son has grown up.

Developing coping strategies

Traditionally there has existed a tension between the strategies and tactics adopted by parents and those preferred by professionals. But parents need to be encouraged and empowered to develop the coping strategies which are best for them. The challenge to professionals is in helping parents to develop those tactics which will enable the strategies to work.

We have seen that mothers and fathers differ in the pace and context in which they adjust to their disabled child. The fact that parents have lived with a diagnosis or prognosis for their child for a long time does not mean that their initial feelings of shock, grief and anxiety are healed. The memories which they have of learning about their child's disability will remain very real and very detailed. Under every stiff upper lip there is a wobbly chin. Most parents who display a calm and controlled exterior will be struggling with turmoil within. Rarely will parents have 'totally come to terms' with their child's difficulties. Many will live their lives in the hope that the diagnosis was wrong and it may well be that this hope is what sustains them.

These words speak of the chronic sorrow still felt eighteen years after twins died: 'Maybe it seems unreasonable but all I wanted was for the experts to recognise our rights as parents to receive the very best help available for the twins and not to deny us the hope of a miracle.'

Professionals who work with parents long after their child's diagnosis should not make assumptions that, because a family has been coping for some time, they are not in need of constant support. The coping strategies which families learn to adopt and the skills they acquire need to be acknowledged.

All parents will need:
- Continued support in adjusting to their emotional and psychological reactions.
- Assistance in seeking professional support.
- Support in recouping their physical strength.
- Assistance in ensuring benefits and resources to meet their needs.
- Adequate information at each stage of their child's development.

Whilst emotional support is vital for parents, there is an increasing understanding of the importance of honest and accurate information at each stage of their child's life. This will include:

- Information about their child's disability.
- Information about the consequences of the disability for the child's short-term and long-term development.
- Helping parents to understand the information which is given to them.
- Helping parents to understand the information within the context of their family and life style.
- Help in setting realistic and meaningful targets for their child.
- Help in contacting parents of children with similar disabilities.
- Knowledge about rights and benefits including medicine, education, respite care and financial support.
- Helping parents to recognise and to celebrate their parenting skills.

Siblings

With the exception of the mother or primary carer, siblings are likely to have more contact with the brother or sister with the disability than any other person. As in the case of mothers, fathers and grandparents, literature which relates to siblings has tended to concentrate on the negative and harmful effects of a brother or sister with disabilities (Seligman and Darling 1989, Simeonsson and McHale 1981). More recently however the research of Meyer and Vadasy (1997), Powell and Gallagher (1993), Hornby (1994) and have paved the way for a consideration of 'opportunities' experienced by brothers and sisters of people with special educational needs.

Opportunities of brothers and sisters of siblings with disabilities:
- An appreciation of their own good health.
- Loyalty and advocacy.
- Pride.
- Increased maturity.
- Insight into disability.   (Based on Meyer and Vadasy 1997)

Gascoigne (1995) includes the needs and difficulties of siblings of children with disabilities in her discussion concerning what she terms day-to-day life with a special needs child. She acknowledges that where a family has a member with special needs, this affects all the family. Of particular note is her belief that siblings may reach social maturity later, a view shared by Atkinson and Crawford (1995) who write about less frequent social opportunities for brothers and sisters of disabled children. Additionally, some brothers and sisters may isolate themselves from their peers, fearing they will be bullied or teased. This opinion is however vehemently dismissed by Hornby (1994) who writes: 'Siblings of children with disabilities tend to be more insightful and tolerant of other's difficulties, to be more certain of their goals in life, to demonstrate greater social competence, and to develop a maturity beyond their years.'

Children are not immune from perceiving the anxieties and stress which their parents are experiencing. Neither do they leave behind that awareness when they themselves go to school. Whilst it would be unwise to suggest that all siblings will themselves have special needs as a result of their family experience, teachers should be aware that their academic performance, self-esteem and social development may be effected.

What can teachers do?
- Be aware of family structures.
- Be aware of anxieties both expressed and unexpressed.
- Be aware that siblings may have special needs in their own right.

Throughout this book it has been advocated that good communication is a key note in supporting people who are enduring loss, change and grief in their lives. This principle applies to siblings who may feel isolated from the family if they perceive that their parents and other family members are making greater endeavours on behalf of their brother or sister.

Feelings of rivalry and resentment exist between all siblings from time to time, but where a disabled child in a family is a focus of attention the feelings of other children can be overwhelming, combining jealousy, hatred and a sense of injustice (Meyer and Vadasy 1997). The expectations of siblings' parents about their academic achievements in relation to that of brothers or sisters can also cause distress. Leder (1991) makes a plea for parents to value their children for who they are and not to over-value the scholastic performance of one family member to the detriment of another.

Stress seems to be more likely in the case of terminal illness or life-threatening conditions. Indeed it is not uncommon for children in the family to blame themselves for their brother's or sister's ill health.

Natasha, aged 13, told me: 'It was probably my fault you see. I was the one who wanted to go to Disney World. It was when we were there that my brother got sick. If we hadn't gone we probably could have got help sooner.'

Another brother felt that his robust physique would have stood him in better stead during ill health than his sister's tiny frame.

When the cancer gets really bad and she can't eat any more and she's too sick to keep the tubes in her, she probably won't last very long. I lifted her into her buggy the other day and she was no heavier than our spaniel.

As in the case of siblings of physically ill children or those who are life-limited or life-threatened, it is vital that children receive honest and open information and reassurance that they are in no way to blame (Murray and Jampolsky 1982). Where a sibling has a genetic condition, information should be made available as brothers and sisters grow older and certainly before they reach child-bearing age (Murphy 1979, Hindmarch 1993). Later in life, if adult siblings take over the responsibility for a brother or sister with a disability, they may find themselves struggling to communicate with support services who often lack expertise in communicating to adult carers other than parents.

What do siblings of brothers and sisters with disabilities need?
- Information to satisfy their own curiosity.
- Information to share with their peers.
- Enhanced access to information, particularly if the disabled sibling has a genetic disorder.
- Reassurance that they were in no way to blame for the disability.
- To be involved in any long term discussions about the future of the disabled sibling.
- Opportunities to share concerns with their peer group.
- Open and honest communication.
- Opportunities to spend time alone with their parents.

Grandparents

Illness, impairment and disability have powerful and often negative meanings attached to them. For many grandparents their grandchild with special needs will be their first close encounter with disability. Like parents they may feel ill equipped and challenged as they grapple with their own emotions.

Much of the literature concerning the role of the extended family when a child has a disability, has concentrated on the supportive role of grandparents (Mirfin-Veitch and Bray 1997, Sandler et al. 1995, Sonnek 1986). However, there are also those grandparents who, for whatever reason, create more stresses rather than alleviating tensions in families (George 1988, Seligman and Darling 1989). Many grandparents feel their grandchildren secure a future for the family tradition and heritage (Roos 1978). When a child with a disability is born into a family the equilibrium is disturbed. Meyer (1993) describes grandparents' emotional responses and the development of coping strategies as being closely allied to those of parents. Indeed the grief experience may well have a negative effect on their ability to support the grandchild's parents, a factor described by Meyer and Vadasy (1986) as 'dual' or 'double grief'. Pieper (1976) describes relationship problems particularly between paternal grandmothers and daughter-in-laws which often lead to family breakdown.

> When my son phoned me from the hospital to tell us James had been born, I knew something was wrong but I wrongly assumed that they had had another girl and he was disappointed. Then he told me James had spina bifida and my whole world fell apart. Selfishly I wondered how you took a handicapped grandson fishing or to watch the match when the team played at home. I just didn't know what to say except 'That's hard on you.' Years later I realised we had been so wound up in our own loss we hadn't been able to give my son and daughter-in-law the support they needed.

Parents in another family described how the grandparents had been the source of immense strength to them:

> I would never have coped without Phil's mother [husband's mother]). She was wonderful. Her sense of determination that we would win through supported us greatly. But she never expected too much of us. She has seen me howling and unable to cope in the morning and come over and sorted us out while Phil was at work. By the time he had come home everything had seemed OK on the surface, and all the shopping and washing and ironing had been done into the bargain.

This supportive approach has a powerful impact on how parents and other extended family members cope (Vadasy *et al.* 1986, Fewell and Meyer 1986). In addition, regular contact with supportive grandparents enhances parents' coping strategies (Mirfin-Veitch and Bray 1997).

Godparents

In a small-scale enquiry Brown (1998) found the supportive role of godparents has also been noted, especially since it seems a large proportion of both godmothers and godfathers are chosen because of their proven commitment to the family as godparents of older siblings or because they have professional expertise within the field of disability.

Alexandra writes:

> When Julie was born I found it hard to be sociable to my friends and my family. But Natalie was different. She never once told me it wasn't as bad as seemed at first. Neither did she tell me to pull myself together. The greatest gift she has ever given me is to hold me tight and to say 'It's tough and it hurts, but give me the chance and I'll support you every inch of the way'. Twenty two years on, she has never let me down.

Another father of a young baby with cerebral palsy wrote:

As a couple his godparents are fantastic. They have baled us out again and again. They know we trust them so we trust ourselves to them too. It's not just Charlie that gets the looking after. Sometimes at the weekend there's a ring at the doorbell and there they are, with dinner for two ready to put in the oven. Occasionally there's a bottle of wine too!

Gascoigne (1995) says, 'Parents rarely come to terms with their child's difficulties'. She then poses the question, should they? Coming to terms she believes may mean giving in and accepting the best they can expect; to believe that progress will be hampered. Whatever the circumstances parents feel conflicting emotions.

Roos (1978) describes these as:

disillusionment: parents invest hopes for the future in their children.

aloneness: bonding and relationships may be more difficult for parents to establish with their child.

vulnerability: the vulnerability experienced in childhood may be re-kindled in parents at the time their child's disability is diagnosed.

inequality: parents' perception of injustice and unfairness in what has happened may lead to a feeling of inequality.

insignificance: disability may shatter perceptions of rewarding parenthood.

past orientation: the future as a parent of a disabled child may be uncertain. Parents may focus on the past or the present.

loss of immortality: facing one's own mortality may be hampered by not being able to invest in the future through a child with a disability. This may be particularly so if the child is an only child.

Adapting to grief

It is neither easy nor wise to attempt to delineate a time scale for parents or extended family members adapting to grief. The time involved will vary, but as with other major losses the process may take up to two years. Crucial to adaptation is the way in which professionals support families and allow them to come to terms with what has happened. The phases are not clearly defined and often parents speak of the confusion they experience as they struggle with a range of emotions. Experiencing an emotion in one phase does not indicate that the previous stage has been mastered. Grief comes and goes like the wave of the ocean.

Some theorists have questioned phased models of adaptation (Blacher 1984). Certainly I have worked with people who have been exceedingly distressed if they have perceived that they have regressed from a later stage of adaptation to an earlier one. This has been particularly prevalent where phases have been described like the horizontal rungs of a ladder.

Scepticism of the adaptation process has led some writers to suggest that the 'chronic sorrow' which families experience becomes an integral part of their emotional and psychological make up (Judd 1989, Max 1985).

The experiences of twelve families with a child with Profound and Multiple Learning Difficulties

One way of obtaining information about how grief and disability affects families is to study how parents cope. I obtained information through a very small sample of twelve families where a child with PMLD had been born during the previous five years. All the children with disabilities had either a brother or a sister in mainstream primary education. All families had two parents living at home, and informal interviews took place with both parents present.

I asked four categories of questions:

- Emotional responses at the time of diagnosis.
- Behaviour changes noticed in self or partner.
- Changes in lifestyle compared with that before the birth of the child with disabilities.
- Experiences of conflict within the family (including extended family) and in the local community.

The tables which follow (Tables 4.1 and 4.2) outline the most commonly described changes in the families adapting to a child with profound and multiple learning difficulties.

Most parents will respond to the news of their child's disability with shock and then pass through a number of stages until they have achieved adaptation.

Emotional Responses	Behavioural Changes	Change in Lifestyle	Conflict within Family and Local Community
• Sad • Shocked • Scared • Unprepared • Angry • Disbelieving	• Anxiety about own health • Sleep disturbance • Fear of developing illness • Inability to concentrate • Over dependency on employed work as an 'escape' • Eating disorders/alcohol or tobacco dependency • Over protectiveness of other siblings • Psychosomatic illness • Depression	• Changed emphasis on domestic activities • Decreased social opportunities • Increased dependence on extended family • Decreased time with family members living in the same household • Financial worries • Fewer holidays • Trying to provide stability for the future	• Spouse or partner • Professionals • Other family members • Neighbours • Siblings' school friends/peer group

Table 4.1 Adapting to a child with profound and multiple learning difficulties

Shock →	Denial →	Anger →	Sadness →	Detachment →	Reorganisation →	Adaptation
→	→	→	→	→	→	→
confusion	disbelief	blame	despair	empty	realism	reconciliation
→	→	→	→	→	→	→
numbness	protest	guilt	grief	meaningless	hope	coming to terms
→	→		→	→		→
disorganisation	disillusionment		depression	insignificance		plans for the future
→	→		→	→		
helplessness	vulnerability		aloneness	inequality		
→						
overwhelming loss						

Table 4.2 The sequence of reactions, emotions and responses

At each stage in the adaptation process parents experience overwhelming emotional responses. These emotions will be experienced at different levels of intensity by different people.

Liz, the mother of a baby son born with PMLD and a life-limited condition eloquently describes in the following pages her experience from the time of Joseph's birth to his death.

The miracle I choose to hang on to

Our son, Joseph, was born on 2 July 1993 and died just twenty five and a half days later. Please God, it is the worst thing that will ever happen to us because I am not sure that we have the strength to survive anything like that again. This does not mean that I have become careful to the point of paranoia with our twenty one month old daughter, Amy. It would serve no purpose and she must be allowed to live her life to the full, unhindered by over-zealous efforts to protect her. The whole experience brought home with a vengeance that life is precious and fragile and that we should value a life, not simply in terms of its length, but more by the quality of it.

And there is the rub where Joseph was concerned. From very early in the pregnancy, I felt that all was not well with him. Once born, it was blatantly obvious that he had a number of problems and I knew, without any doubt, that he would not survive very long. From that moment all I wanted to do was to take him home and shower him with love. Instead he was removed to the hospital where he underwent extensive tests, all of which returned normal results and left the specialists baffled. Granted, not all the investigations were painful or invasive but knowing he would die, and soon, made his stay in the hospital a living nightmare for me. My partner, Mike, never gave up hope and, scientist that he is, knowing what was wrong and what had caused Joseph's problems made our son's absence from us almost tolerable for him.

Friends asked whether if we had had answers, would I have looked on that aspect of his life differently. I doubt it. I felt, and still do, that he became a guinea pig for this abstract ideal we call medical advance which ran away with us long ago. It seems the medical profession now feels compelled to save lives, just because it can, rarely hesitating to ask if it should. That said, in another scenario, we may be grateful for any and all medical know-how. Every case is unique but in Joseph's it was entirely inappropriate to subject him to so much and in so doing, starve him of one of the few things young babies are known to be aware of – loving human contact from his mother.

If I have any bitterness at all, it centres on the proportion of his life Joseph spent at the hospital as against the time I had just holding him and loving him. And that the medical profession has become so clever that some of their members seem to believe that knowledge can replace a mother's instinct. It was that instinct which provided the only positive element in the whole sad business.

The hospital finally conceded that Joseph's case was hopeless. Whatever had caused his problems and whatever the extent of those problems we would probably never know. A bulbar palsy was diagnosed: the medical name for an inability to swallow. It is in itself a fatal condition and acknowledging this he was at last allowed to return to our local hospital, with weeks or months, but certainly not years to live. We were permitted to say what could and could not be done for him and were faced with dilemmas concerning what treatments and practices were prolonging his life and his suffering as against those which were making him as comfortable as possible.

He had been at the local hospital just about a week when I felt he was deteriorating. Physically there was nothing to confirm this suspicion. Medically, I was told, there was no change and that, if anything, his oxygen requirement, particularly when I was with him, had decreased. By the second evening of concern, I knew that he would die very soon. At 2 am on 28 July I brought our son home. At five minutes to seven the same morning he died quietly, and oh! so peacefully in my arms.

Those last hours were wonderful, precious – almost idyllic. I had had a picture, almost a vision, as to how I wanted his end to be but feared I was being naive in the detail of that hope. I knew that he was at high risk of choking and dying suddenly in my absence, yet I was clear that I did not want him home to play 'happy families'; indulging in a charade that Joseph had completed our number only to look back at that time with unbearable sadness.

There will always be sadness but for me it is bearable because the end was all that I had hoped for. The house was quiet as we snuggled up in bed together and there were no distractions as I poured my love over and into him. His passing was not ugly or frightening; he seemed literally just to 'let go' and I felt inner peace and tranquillity as I too, let him go.

If I look at the events of his life as a journey to that final time together, then I can live with them. There is nothing I can do to change the facts of his tragic life or the dark days at the first hospital but I thank God for the miracle of bringing him home and for the loveliness of our last hours together. It is that miracle that I choose to hang on to.

Chapter 5

Children in Distress

Refugees

The number of children living in accommodation for homeless families has increased rapidly during the last two decades. Bradshaw (1990) estimates that it has in fact doubled in this period. Indeed there are at present (1998) an estimated 25,000 refugee children in UK schools. Teachers have a pivotal role to play in supporting such children and their families. Often refugee children have had horrendous experiences and they arrive in schools disorientated, shocked and traumatised. Many travel to Great Britain by air where asylum has been sought at the airport. Since the passage of the 1993 Asylum and Immigration (Appeals) Act, about 5 per cent of asylum seekers have been granted full refugee status which protects them from being returned to their country of origin. In addition, refugee status also gives a person the right to bring their family to the country of settlement.

Amongst the main groups of refugees in Great Britain are Turkish Qurds, Ghanaians, Nigerians, Sierra Leonians, Ethiopians, Sudanese, Ugandans, Somalis, Zairians, Sri Lankan Tamils and Iraqis. The Refugee Council estimates there were in the region of 300 unaccompanied children who arrived in 1993. Amongst these children are those who witnessed the murder or violent death of a family member. However, the families of most unaccompanied refugee children are still alive but maintaining contact is often difficult or impossible.

Refugee children also come from countries where the education system may be very different from that in the country in which they arrive. Some may have had an interrupted education because of war or unrest in their own country. Almost without exception a refugee child will have experienced a multiplicity of different stressful events. Most children cope with the multiple stresses of being a refugee but some remain psychologically vulnerable and a few children manifest disturbed behaviour. Whatever their experiences there will be a culmination of loss, trauma and change.

Loss

Children who have lost their parents or primary carers, siblings or extended family, will not only have lost their roots in their homeland, but the security of the people they were emotionally involved with. They may be bereft of the only home they have ever known and have few or no personal possessions or favourite toys. Suddenly they have to adapt to new people, surroundings and patterns of life.

Trauma

Many children are the victims of war where their homes have been destroyed and their parents may have been abducted, tortured, imprisoned, or killed. Often they will have witnessed first hand, rape, famine and material deprivation, and have no language with which to talk about what has happened. Like unwanted baggage they carry these memories until they can find some way of coping.

Change

Refugee children may experience major changes such as climate, housing, education, diet and language. Their status in society may be different and they will often be vulnerable to bullying and teasing.

Supporting refugee children

One of the most important things teachers can do is to talk to distressed children, listen to what they say and take their communication seriously. It is essential to develop good communication and a pastoral curriculum as well as providing safe places for children. Starting a new school can be a very frightening experience for many refugees. British schools are large and noisy. A refugee child may feel lost and may speak no English when they first arrive and they may have no friends. Although a child may be able to cope during lesson time, break time can be overwhelming.

When working with refugee children it is important that we do not make assumptions about their experiences or that we label them all as being different or traumatised. All children will experience loss, change and grief in their lives and whilst we should not underestimate their trauma, each child will react differently to these experiences. Most people will experience strong emotional responses immediately after distressing events. The way in which a refugee child adapts to his or her experience will largely depend on:

- the quality of life experience before becoming a refugee;
- the duration and intensity of the trauma and any previous traumas;
- her ability to understand the changes;
- the amount of support available in the new environment including housing, education and opportunities to express feelings;
- contact or communication with other people from her home country and friendship in the new place.

A minority of refugee children will demonstrate disturbed or challenging behaviour as a result of being unhappy or distressed. This might be shown as:

• lethargy; a lack of energy and being withdrawn;
• lacking concentration, day-dreaming and feeling restless;
• regression in educational progress or losing acquired skills;
• aggression, anger or irritability mirroring the violence they have experienced;
• repetitive re-living of violent events through play, drawings, night-terrors;
• disturbed sleep, enuresis;
• crying and feeling overwhelming sadness;
• nervousness or fear of new situations;
• inability to form or sustain relationships.

Unaccompanied children

Amongst refugee children who are particularly vulnerable and at risk are those who arrive in Britain alone. Some families send their children to another country because they believe their lives to be threatened. Other children have become separated from their parents or they are orphans because their primary carers have been killed or murdered. Research by Rutter (1994) reveals that in at least 25 countries throughout the world children under 16 make up a significant percentage of national armies, guerrilla groups or both. Parents may send their child away to prevent forced recruitment and the number of male children exceeds female children for this reason.

A minority of unaccompanied children arrive escorted by family friends or agents and others come with older siblings. At present the British legal system does not discriminate between refugee adults and children, and therefore unaccompanied children often encounter the same procedures applying for political asylum. Many young people are unaware of their rights and entitlements which include being kept informed about decisions being made on their behalf.

Under the Children Act (1989) local authorities have responsibility for the welfare of 'children in need' up to the age of 16. However, some refugee organisations believe that the needs of children are not being met. These needs include support appropriate to the child's race, culture, creed and linguistic group.

A large percentage of unaccompanied refugee children will be cared for in residential settings or they will be fostered. A small number will be adopted.

How can schools help?
• Provide a sympathetic friend, preferably one who speaks the same first language.
• Give as much visual support in learning as possible.
• Ensure that teacher and children know each other's names and are able to say them clearly.

- Provide opportunities for children to make verbal contact with other pupils.
- Provide a group where children are best able to be involved in their learning tasks.
- Encourage children to ask for help when they do not understand work.

Divorce

And the King said: Fetch me a sword. And they brought a sword for the King. And the King said: Divide the living child in two, and give half to the one, and half to the other. (Kings 3 v. 23–25).

Robinson (1991) describes divorce as a slow and turbulent bereavement. However, she says it differs from bereavement as a result of death which is generally ascribed to fate rather than fault. Divorce nearly always leaves a legacy of anger, guilt and shame where individuals lose their self-esteem and their lives are turned upside-down and inside-out.

Divorce is a longitudinal process that begins long before family break-up and continues long after it. Over the last decade the number of families headed by a single parent has increased by over 70 per cent to 1.3 million. Lone parent families now make up 19 per cent of all families in the UK and it is estimated that about one in five children live in a single parent family (Rowntree 1988). Marital breakdown is the single most important determinant of one parent families but the stereotypical perception that it is only the mother who is capable of bringing up young children is changing (Ayalon and Flasher 1993). If recent trends continue, more than a third of new marriages will end within twenty years and four out of ten will ultimately end in divorce (Rowntree 1998). This means for children under 16 years of age, one in four will experience parental divorce. As a result many of these young people will be disadvantaged both in the short term and the long term.

Research into the impact of divorce and separation on children is not conclusive since there has been a failure to distinguish between separation as a process and separation as an event. When parents divorce, their legal status is one of dissolution but for the children the situation may be heart-breakingly difficult (see Kim's drawing, Figure 5.1). Many recent researchers strive to describe divorce. On the one hand there are those who pursue the social processes of divorce, whilst on the other there are those who seek to describe the psychological process. When families are divided their private sorrows become public issues.

Janet, aged 16, said:

It would have been so much better if my parents had explained what was going on. The split all happened without telling me anything. Once I answered the door and a courier gave me a whole load of papers. My mum wasn't in – she was working, so I had to sign for them. Next day I took them out of mum's handbag and read them. It said my mum had

Figure 5.1 My heart fell down. Kim, aged five

custody of me but my dad had access. I worried all that night my dad would come back and get me then and my parents would fight.

The seminal work of Bowlby (1969) revolutionised ideas and understanding about making and breaking affectionate bonds. Weiss (1975) draws on Bowlby's work in his research on marital separation. He likens the process of ending a marriage and becoming single again, in inter-relational terms of the individual with important attachment figures. His work describes the erosion of love, the persistence of attachment, the decision to separate, as well as subsequent phases including the effects of separation on children, relatives and friends.

Darren wrote the following in his school diary:

One weekend when my dad was working my mum took us to my gran's and left us there. Dad came home on Sunday and all his things were gone. I didn't know what was going on. Mum got a divorce without my dad knowing. I still see my dad at weekends but he has got a new wife and my mum is living with my new dad so it will never be a family again.

A more recent study by Berman (1988) describes attachments and distress as separate constructs and this is a theory which is applied by Ahrons and

Bowman (1982) to divorce. Research undertaken by Davis and Murch (1992) shows that about 13 per cent of couples reconcile after they have in fact filed for divorce.

Parental responsibility and the Children Act

The Children Act (1989) is based on the belief that both parents should be involved in the upbringing of their children. Underpinning this is the philosophy that each parent should behave responsibly towards the children. 'Parental responsibility' is defined in the Act as: *all the rights, duties, powers, responsibilities and authority which by law a parent of a child has in relation to the child and his property.* (Section 3:1). This emphasis on responsibility exists primarily for the benefit of the child until he or she is 18 years of age. After a separation or divorce both parents automatically continue to have responsibility. An unmarried mother has parental responsibility but this may also be assumed by the father through agreement with the mother or through the law courts. Other people including step parents, relatives, co-habitees and foster parents may legally acquire responsibility by court action.

Step families

According to Rimmer (1991), one in three marriages are remarriages for at least one partner, and recent figures indicate that about half of these is likely to end in divorce. Step families are often the victims of negative opinion thought to be dominated by wicked step mothers who rule the home and terrorise the children, or step fathers who endanger innocent young girls. According to Robinson (1991) all step families have to negotiate their roles in an 'ad hoc way often during periods of considerable stress and in isolation'.

Step families have been described in a variety of ways. Shulman (1981) refers to *re-constituted* familes; Wald (1981) to *blended* families and Ihinger-Tallman and Pasley (1987) as *re-married* families. Because the majority of mothers retain custody of their children following divorce, most step parent households are those with a step father.

Visher and Visher (1988) have distinguished some of the common characteristics of step families:

- *Complex family structures* resulting in ambiguous boundaries between the families.
- *Stress* and unresolved problems following the divorce or death of a biological parent.
- *Functional integration problems* taking up to two years depending on the age and sex of the children at the time the step family is formed.
- *Severance of relationships* which are frequent in step families and common in step father households. These cut offs may be partial, temporary or permanent.
- *Continual transition* and movement of children between households.

- *Less cohesiveness or attachment* of children to step parents.
- *Variety of family management structures* especially where there is diversity in access or custody arrangements.
- *Unrealistic expections* as the step family strives to be a nuclear family.
- *Non-familiarity with the past history of the family* often referred to as 'culture shock'.
- *Difficulty in communication* as members strive to build up shared beliefs or where former relationships intrude on the privacy of the step family.
- *Loyalty conflicts* where family members have psychological bonds to different people.

Children are likely to experience disruption of their roots followed perhaps by the arrival of step siblings or half siblings. Where children have had experience of living in a single parent household they may also experience the loss of their primary carer's sole attention.

In many step families living space is at a premium and step children or half siblings may impinge on the territory of the former family. Parents who remarry often believe that because they have chosen to be together the children in the family will feel the same, although this may be far from the case. Furthermore, many formerly married couples have not emotionally divorced from their previous marriage prior to a new relationship. Parents may remarry or live together very soon after divorce which can complicate the mourning processes of children, not least because many have not given up yearning that their birth parents will get together again. It may not be until one parent remarries that they are able to grieve for the loss of their original family. Therefore divorce requires major reorganisation in the extended family. The differing jealousies of step family members may reveal deep uncertainties and unresolved emotional baggage. Although there seems to have been virtually no research into the role of grandparents during the process of divorce and remarriage, they often play a very significant role in the family network. Indeed during the tempestuous stages of divorce grandparents may provide stability which parents are unable to realise.

There are no records of the number of children of remarrying parents so the statistics for children with step parents can only be estimated. However, the Report of the Consultative Group on Ministry among Children (1995) Section 1:8 estimates that by the year 2000 only half of all children will spend their childhood with their natural parents. Webb (1994) states that at present there are at least 900,000 step families in the UK.

The effects of family break-up

The effects of family break-up are manifold and extend far beyond the emotional and social well-being of children. They may include:

- *legal proceedings* relating to divorce or separation;
- *economic changes* including the division of the home into two independent units and child support payments;

- *changed roles in parental responsibilities* (although according to the Children Act both parents legally retain responsibility towards their children);
- *changed social status* and adapting to 'single' parent;
- *severance of family relationships*.

Each family member must adapt at his or her own pace and with different degrees of involvement. The frequency of contact with families seems to be less important than the quality (Rowntree 1998).

For children, verbal and physical conflict between two people they love is confusing and upsetting. All families are different, and so are the ways in which they break up, but whatever the circumstances of the separation, children may experience a sense of loss, betrayal and anger. Almost always they want their parents to stay together and they may feel despair at their inability to influence what is happening.

The following children tell their own stories:

I didn't know anything was wrong. It was a big shock when they divorced. It was as if all my childhood had been a lie.

My mum told me they were happy once but I only remember the fighting.

Our mum used to drink. Sometimes she hurt us and once she broke her arm when she fell down the stairs. Our dad tried to get help for her but she used to swear at him and hit him when he talked to her. So we had to get a divorce. Now I'll never see my mum again because she lives rough. But we are going to get an au pair for my brother and sister. I am looking forward to that. I never told my friends what it was like, I was too ashamed.

Whilst it is dangerous to generalise about children's responses due to differences in personality, gender, family structure etc. the following are not uncommon:

Early years (5–7 years)

Young children often show frightened, anxious and clinging behaviour which may be accompanied by attention seeking. The younger they are, the more likely they are to think they were responsible for what has happened to their parents. However, the younger the child, the less likely they are to conceal emotional responses to distress. They reason that if one parent has left them, then so can the other, so they set out to try to reunite them through behaviour such as becoming ill or regressing to younger behaviour. Some will attempt to test their parents' love for them and may withdraw from close contact with one parent out of loyalty to the other. Patterns of play are often characterised by desperate searching and in some cases poor social skills.

7–11 years

Older children are more likely to react less negatively to the news their parents are divorcing. At this age, although children may be more able to appreciate other people's points of view, most still think that their parents should be capable of sorting things out. When the latter does not happen they may become very angry and show sullen or disruptive behaviour. Feelings of deprivation may be shown by an insatiable desire for food or material belongings. See-saw behaviours such as those that are radically different between home and school are very common. The nature of children's responses relates to their age and previous experience of loss and change in their lives, together with the stage of development that they had reached at the time of the divorce. Kelly (1988) describes role-reversal of children of nine years and upwards who may attempt to become a nurturing parent.

Becky told me: 'My dad and mum divorced and my mum got married again but it didn't last, so I have been through two divorces so far.'

12 plus years

Older children may deeply resent what has happened and in an attempt to place blame on their parents they may cut themselves off, manifesting anger and hostility. Often they seek support outside the home. One child said:

> When my dad went away I lost the dad I had known all my life. He got a new partner. When he was with her he tried to show her how fond of me he was. If I met him alone he made it quite clear I was just a financial and emotional burden.

Relationships with parents often fluctuate wildly and loyalty conflicts are frequently characterised by deep anger. Nord (1989) believes 'that divorce takes a far heavier toll on children's self-image and their abilty to sustain male and female relationships than has previously been believed'. Furthermore there seems to be increasing evidence that boys and girls are affected differently; the long-term effects on boys apparently being greater. Some young people may adopt a surrogate parental role in relation to younger siblings which may complicate the normal development of peer relationships.

Whatever the age of children they will have to master tasks in order that they are able to adjust the the divorce. These will include:

• acknowledging the reality of marital separation;
• disengaging from parental conflict;
• resolution of loss;
• resolving anger and self-blame;
• acceptance of the permanence of divorce;
• achieving realistic hope about their own future relationships.

What do children need from their parents?

- Honest and open information.
- Reassurance that they will be cared for.
- Reassurance that they were not responsible.
- Consistent and predictable routines.
- Access to both parents wherever possible or where this is not possible contact by phone, letter, etc.
- Adults who make decisions and who do not expect them to take sides.

For any divorcing couple there are always two stories – the husband's and the wife's. Both parties attempt to make their own sense of what is happening. It is almost impossible to shield children from the distress and anger which they feel and research (Walczak and Burns 1984) suggests that parental grief responses render parents virtually unable to consider the implications of their separation for their children. Sometimes both partners remain in the matrimonial home, each pressurising and manipulating the other to move out. In addition the extended family may begin to try to make sense of what is happening and unwillingly they may take sides with one of the parents.

Research shows that the crucial time in the parent/child relationships are the first few weeks after one parent leaves home when the attachment between adults and children need to be reinforced, especially in the case of non-custodial fathers. The quality of parenting often deteriorates during the divorce for a period of up to two years (Kelly 1988).

Children of divorcing parents need to understand what is happening to them and ultimately to come to terms with the breakdown of the marriage. Often the realisation of what has gone wrong comes as a great shock. The ways in which they can best be helped will largely depend on the skills of their parents to continue to support them emotionally, and to maintain the child/parent bond.

The effects of divorce on children are related to their age and stage of individual development at the time of the marital breakdown. The long-term effects on children have been described by Wallerstein and Blakeslee (1989). These include:

- delayed emotional and social development if relationships with both parents are not maintained;
- diminished capacity for parenting;
- increased danger of unrelinquished compounded grief from subsequent bereavements;
- over-burdening responsibility to role-play absent parents.

Divided families at school

Often schools are expected to take over the nurturing role formerly provided by home. At other times they bear the brunt of physical or verbal aggression from parents. Whatever the situation, schools may be the only consistent and reliable element in a child's life which is otherwise uncertain and unpredictable.

According to Thompson *et al.* (1984) and Noy (1991) divorce has six major adverse effects on a child's schooling:

- decline in performance in literacy, language and numeracy;
- changes in ability to communicate;
- inability to form relationships with peers/adults which may instigate teasing or bullying;
- lack of concentration;
- aggression;
- reluctance to disclose the stress experienced.

What can schools do?

- Update information on children's home circumstances regularly.
- Keep contact with home but avoid criticising either parent.
- Establish procedures for keeping both parents informed of their child's progress and of school events.
- Reassure children that their responses to the family crisis are normal.
- Reassure children that whatever happens in their parents' relationship it was not their fault.
- Keep school routines as constant as possible.
- Understand that changed behaviour may be the result of loss, disappointment and change
- Plan a curriculum which makes reference to a variety of family structures.

Despite the increase in divorce and remarriage and children who will live in step parents' families, there is very little that has been written to support those teachers who will be caring for children who will spend approximately two-thirds of their waking life in school.

In school it is inevitable that children will manifest emotional stress related to what is happening at home. Typically they will feel:

- *bewilderment* about what is happening, especially if parents tell them half-truths;
- *powerless* in the midst of the struggles between parents;
- *divided loyalties* as a direct result of being caught up in the cross fire of parental demands;
- *loss of self-esteem* because children perceive themselves as 'different'.

Children tell us quite simply and clearly that the effects of divorce are very great on them. There seems to be a need for them to be given information and for children to keep contact with both parents. Without exception children are fearful of verbal and physical aggression between their parents but they often try to hide this. For some children they perceive a stigma about divorce, trying to hide what is happening from their peer group.

Prisoners' children

Prisoners' children have been referred to as 'forgotten victims' (Shaw 1989), 'orphans of justice' (Shaw 1992) or as being 'sentenced by association' (Blake 1991). It is estimated that in England and Wales in excess of 125,000 children a year are affected by a parent in prison (NACRO 1993, Save the Children 1997). These numbers are increasing as the result of the conviction and custody of people for non-violent crimes. The plight of prisoners' families in the United Kingdom has been a matter of concern for a number of years (Morris 1967, Matthews 1983, Light 1989) but save for the work of Shaw (1986, 1987, 1989, 1992) and more recently Ramsden (1998), little is known about the impact of custodial sentences on children.

**PRISON STATISTICS 1996
(ENGLAND AND WALES)**
(Average components of prison population)

Adult Males	34,600
Adult Females	2,260
Male Remand	11,000
Male Young Offenders	6,490

Source HMSO (1996)

The legal rights of prisoners' children

The rights of children of imprisoned parents are worthy of consideration, yet at the time of writing, this category of young people does not have any legal benefits or entitlements in the United Kingdom. It is only when a child is born in prison and where a mother is sentenced whilst a child is very young that the child's needs will be taken into account (Cooklin 1989). However, the United Nations Convention on the Rights of the Child provides a helpful framework in setting the rights of prisoners' children.

Article 9 states:

> ... shall respect the rights of the child who is separated from one or both parents to maintain personal relations and direct contact with both parents on a regular basis, except if it is contradictory to the terms of the child's best interest.

This was endorsed by the Children Act (1989) and the Department of Health (1989) which state that whenever children are separated from a parent for whatever reason, family links should be actively maintained through visits or other forms of contact.

In 1994 the Children's Rights Development Unit undertook to review how law, policy and practice in the United Kingdom complied with the standards set out in the United Nations Convention. The findings stated that 'the current arrangements failed to take into account children's best interests' (Article 3).

Nearly two decades ago a team of Australian researchers investigating the lives of prisoners' children categorised them according to the type of care they received and the amount of contact they were able to maintain with the imprisoned parent/s (Hounslow *et al.* 1982). The categorisation fell into four discrete areas:

1. Children who remain with one parent or a member of their family and will have some contact with the parent who is imprisoned. The largest number of young people in this category have a father in prison.
2. Children whose circumstances are akin to those of the first group but who maintain little or no contact with the imprisoned parent. Most children in this group have a mother in prison.
3. Children who live in prison with their mother.
4. Children who are placed in care by the welfare system.

In addition there is another category of children about whom very little is known. These are the offspring of juvenile offenders who are themselves in prison (Cadale 1991).

Very little systematic follow up of prisoners' children exists concerning the long-term effects which they encounter, although a study commissioned by the Home Office (Richards *et al.* 1994) confirms the psychological damage to children. The Enquiry found about 30 per cent of imprisoned mothers and fathers thought their children were coping badly. Moore (1992) confirms that few prisoners have any contact with their children's school.

What are the experiences of prisoners' children?

When a parent goes to prison a child may experience:

- loss of contact with familiar people and family members;
- financial hardship;
- stigmatisation from peer group and in some cases adult society;
- loss of their roots through moving home or being taken into care;
- loss of part of their childhood if they become responsible for looking after younger siblings;
- emotional upheaval and tension at home.

Ramsden in a recent publication (1998) says: 'The consensus among agencies working in the field is that when a parent goes to prison the child is also punished.' (p. 25).

One prisoner's partner who was a parent of a child at a special school told me, 'It's like being condemned against yourself. First you have to live with the news your child will never be normal. Then you have to deal with the fact your home and social life is ruined because of no fault of your own.'

Ramsden (1998) describes children's emotional responses to loss of a parent through imprisonment as isolation, guilt, low self-esteem, confusion and frustration. She writes how these feelings may be manifested through:

- bed wetting;
- nightmares;
- temper tantrums;
- aggressive behaviour;
- withdrawal;
- refusing to go to school.

Prison support agencies recommend that children should be told the truth about their imprisoned parent as soon as possible, but parents or carers who are grieving themselves may not feel skilled enough to break the news or to continue caring for children throughout the duration of the sentence.

Children of prisoners frequently become confused because either information is withheld from them or they learn half-truths, from their carers or from people outside the family. Shaw's research (1992) indicates that only about a third of children are told the truth. The remainder are given explanations for absence which relate to working or studying away from home, hospitalisation, or holidays.

Marie is six. She was told her mummy had died. On her birthday she received a card which,, she told me, 'God posted in heaven for my mummy.'

Prisoners' families

In family conflict, it is not always easy to pick the victim – except the children, who are always the victim. Pope (1987b).

Richards (1992) describes the effects which imprisonment has on families and there are some similarities akin to those of parental divorce cited earlier in this chapter. Parents who are preoccupied with their own problems or depressed are generally less good at providing support and extra attention for their children. In addition, because they may feel unable to provide children with straightforward information about the imprisoned person, children's worst fears and fantasies may grow. Together with their families they are often lacking in support because of negative responses from neighbours and the local community. Within the family unit the strains which imprisonment places on relationships may lead to divorce so that a child may bear double disruption and grief. At best, most partnerships will be strained and feelings of bitterness coupled with anxiety and guilt may result in conflict. Even when a sentence is completed there may be a period of readjustment for all family members as they strive to forge new relationships.

Where a family member is in prison those outside may experience:

- poverty through a decline in income;
- increased financial demands (for example providing transport for visits);

- change of roles and responsibilities amongst carers;
- discrimination or hostility from neighbours and the local community;
- upheaval through moving or being re-housed.

They may also feel:

- anger towards the prisoner and a feeling of betrayal on their part;
- confusion and hostility towards authority figures;
- anxiety of behalf of the prisoner;
- concern for the prisoner's welfare;
- frustration that they are unable to offer more support to the prisoner/family;
- a sense of degradation from peers and in some cases professional people.

Children of imprisoned mothers and fathers

It is a world-wide phenomenon that when a woman is sent to prison, she takes her younger children with her. Lloyd (1995).

This statement may have some validity, but it should be remembered that children of imprisoned mothers and fathers are not an homogeneous group any more than any other groupings of children who are victims of loss, change and grief. Shaw (1987) describes the factors which unite prisoners' children as firstly poverty and secondly stigmatisation.

For many children separation from a parent begins at the time of arrest (Blake 1991) and difficulties begin for all family members (McDermott and King 1992). Shaw (1989) writes: 'It is the right of the child to maintain a meaningful relationship with his parent...instead of visits being viewed as the right (or privilege) of the prisoner.' (p. 28).

There are, of course, exceptions to this, for example where a parent is in custody as a result of abusing their child.

Fathers

Shaw (1992) refers to children of imprisoned fathers as 'orphans of justice'. In his study of children of imprisoned fathers in England the author estimated that at the time there were in excess of half a million children under the age of 16 who had experienced incarceration of their father on more than one occasion, a fact confirmed by The Central Statistical Office.

The majority of children of imprisoned fathers are amongst the most socially, financially and educationally deprived young people in Great Britain. Health visitors report that lone mothers are not only coping with their partner in custody but also contending with drug abuse, alcohol or solvent abuse, unemployment, poor housing and health problems (Shaw 1989). Furthermore it is known that these same families may be victims of vindictiveness and viewed with a lack of interest by officialdom and bureaucratic systems. Pope

(1987a) speaks of prison destroying or damaging the paternal image in both fathers and children which in turn seems to provide the impetus for what she calls emotional and marital 'disengagement'.

According to Shaw (1992) the plight of prisoners' children is steadily worsening. Many fathers are being held in remand centres a long way from their families whilst they are awaiting sentence, making meaningful contact almost impossible. In addition the penal system of Great Britain has limited opportunities for home leave of prisoners. Many fathers also leave pregnant partners or wives at the time of their imprisonment. Children whose fathers are imprisoned on short sentences may not be given truthful explanations for his absence, a fact which Monger and Pendleton (1981) describes as having 'disastrous consequences if children discover the reality for themselves'.

Pellegrini's (1992a) unpublished study reveals that children's sense of right and wrong and their moral reasoning has an effect on the way they feel about themselves when a father is imprisoned. As with children's knowledge about life-threatening illness and death, Pelligrini (1992b) maintains that children learn that a parent's absence is due to imprisonment through overheard conversations and other discoveries. The same researcher describes a number of tasks which children of imprisoned fathers need to achieve in order to adjust to the situation. These may be summarised as:

- adjusting to the pattern of prison visits;
- adjusting to unfavourable aspects of prison visits;
- competing with other people for attention from the visitor;
- coming to terms with different emotional feelings during visits;
- coping with responses from peers.

Many children of imprisoned fathers experience bullying and rejection from their peer group (Howard League 1994) and in some cases brothers and sisters are separated whilst they are in care. Generally they suffer poor self-esteem and occasionally (especially amongst black children) a loss of identity (Amera 1992).

Mothers

Several recent studies have focused exclusively on children of imprisoned mothers (Lloyd 1990, Woodrow 1992). The findings reveal that about 5 per cent of imprisoned persons are mothers. A report by NACRO (1994) supports the views of Lloyd and Woodrow, pointing to the fact that the criminal justice system in the United Kingdom discriminates against women, who are less likely to be bailed for offences than their male counterparts. In addition, Wilkinson (1998), in a study of post-release women, concludes that lack of contact by female prisoners with their children jeopardises the chances of families being reunited after release. Even more worrying is the data from the Howard League (1994), which suggests that over 10 per cent of children who have a mother in prison are taken into care.

Little is known about the short- or long-term effect of maternal imprisonment on children who live in the outside community. Woodrow (1992) believes limited published research in this area is indicative of a lack of public awareness. In addition the same author is of the opinion that the statistics for this group of women and children are unlikely to be accurate since mothers are reluctant to divulge the existence of children for fear that they will be taken into care.

The situation for children of imprisoned mothers is often more complex and serious than for children of male prisoners. Because many imprisoned mothers are single parents, children not only lose their principle carer, but they become parentless into the bargain (Casale 1989).

Research demonstrates that the majority of women in prison are at the disadvantaged end of the socio-economic spectrum, with associated poor housing, unemployment and limited parenting skills (Casale 1989, Catan 1989a). Carers of children are likely to be late middle-aged or elderly or, if young, single parents dependent on income support (Catan 1989a) and struggling to function without a formal support network (Shaw 1989).

As well as being separated from their mothers, children are frequently separated from their siblings at the time of imprisonment or if care situations break down. Older siblings may take on the role of looking after younger brothers and sisters (Shaw 1987). It is not uncommon for women to be imprisoned without knowing where their children are (Casale 1989, Posen 1988). Where contact is maintained, crowded and impersonal venues are often the scene of tearful and traumatic visits for children and in some cases children may be introduced to a sibling born during their mother's sentence.

When women return home at the end of their sentence they may do so in greater debt than when they were imprisoned owing to rent arrears and bearing the costs of visits from their children.

In addition, having a criminal record means it is difficult to obtain paid employment and therefore to live independently with the result that women may not be viewed as sufficiently settled to regain custody of their children. Some will attempt to either reestablish relationships with former violent partners or be forced to live in appalling housing. As a result children may be reunited with their mothers in very unsatisfactory circumstances (Wilkinson 1988).

Sian, aged 11, told me he hated going home to his mum because they had to share a bathroom with three other families and there were broken bottles and needles in there. 'Margaret, my foster mum, had a shower and a bath and we could stay in their bathroom as long as we like.'

The characteristics of children of female prisoners have been described by Larman and Aungles (1991).

- Children are less likely to be cared for by a co-parent or another family member.
- Children are less likely to live in a continuous stable environment.

• Children are less likely to visit their mothers regularly.
• Children are less likely to keep in contact by letters and phone calls.

Mothers and babies

White (1989) documents the plights of mothers and babies imprisoned together and babies cared for outside prison. She makes a plea for mothers to be kept out of prison wherever possible. Her views are endorsed by Catan (1989a, 1992) whose research has revealed slower development in babies during their time spent in prison. Generally there may be a greater degree of stability found amongst these babies than those who are placed in care outside the prison, often with a number of people acting as carers. Richards *et al.* (1994) believe mothers separated from their young babies have particular difficulties in sustaining a parental relationship in later life.

It may well be that in the long term, the children of imprisoned mothers are at risk of delinquency and even fending for themselves in later life. The needs of these children are manifold.

What do prisoners' children need?
• Information about their imprisoned parents.
• Help and understanding about what is happening.
• Remaining in familiar surroundings as far as possible.
• Carers who are supported by welfare departments providing practical or financial help.
• Regular and meaningful contact with the imprisoned parent.
• Their rights and needs taken into account before a custodial sentence is given to their parent.
• Ongoing support after the release of their parent.
• Opportunities to be included in decisions which relate to them.
• People who will respect their confidentiality.

The role of the school and children of imprisoned parents

For many children of imprisoned parents, school provides a familiar, consistent and safe place where positive behaviour is rewarded within a commonly agreed framework. At present there is no legal requirement for a child's school to be informed when a parent in sent to prison. Indeed many schools only hear about imprisoned parents as the result of child protection measures, fostering or care arrangements or indirectly through the children themselves.

Things which teachers noticed about children of imprisoned parents
• Changes in behaviour, for example, withdrawal, anger, aggression.
• Changes in personality and mood.
• Lack of concentration.
• Being bullied.
• Appearing withdrawn.

- Appearing upset.
- Antagonism towards authority figures.
- Physical violence.

Prisoners' children may display many of the characteristic changes in behaviour and decline in academic achievement which are similar to children suffering other experiences of loss and change. How children respond is likely to be determined by their age, level of cognitive understanding and experience of loss and change in their life at the beginning of the period of remand or custodial sentence. It is likely that the phase or stages within the period of custody will have profound effects on children. These periods or phases may be summarised as:

- arrest;
- a visit by the child to a remand centre or prison;
- a visit by the imprisoned parent to the place where the child is being cared for;
- the release of a parent from a remand centre or prison;
- discovering or being told about their parent's imprisonment.

What can teachers do?
Ramsden (1998), whilst urging her readers to be cautious regarding the principles of good practice which might apply to the children of all imprisoned parents, makes the following recommendations:

- Listen carefully to what children communicate.
- See the child as an individual with individual needs.
- Be non-judgmental.
- Avoid treating the child as a victim or being over-protective.
- Acknowledge the child's own preferences.
- Don't ask about the crime.
- Reassure the child of support from school and be available for the child as far as possible.

Teachers seem to know about imprisoned parents from a variety of sources. This will include:

- the absence of the parent;
- information told by the child, the carer or the parent to teachers, support staff or other people in school;
- uncharacteristic or deteriorated behaviour;
- unauthorised absences from school.

In a small-scale research project (Brown 1994) teachers were able to identify children in their classes who had either a parent or someone they knew well in prison. The words which follow are exactly as the children responded when they were asked to describe their experiences of prison visits:

Me mum told me sister and me our dad were in hospital. But what she didn't know was we could both read the prison notice above the gates when we went to visit. In any case, you don't get nurses in black uniforms with handcuffs and bunches of keys. Our mum's lies made it more harder when we found out. (Girl aged eleven.)

Visiting me dad is O.K. 'cos you can buy chocolate at the counter before you go to speak to him. (Boy aged seven.)

I hate going to where my dad is. The only good bit is you can play snakes and ladders and ludo. The bad bits are the chairs are hard and the tables are too high. The grown ups in the place make you sit on the chairs. You can't get up and walk around. (Boy aged nine.)

The first time I went to visit my mum it was with my foster parents. My foster mum and I were taken into a room and we had to be searched. I don't know what they expected to find. I mean, it's my real mum who did the crime, not us. (Girl aged fourteen.)

The bad bit is I had to leave my Telytubby doll at the place where you go in. I wanted to show it to my brother. The good bit is my mum always buys us coke and chips on the way home. (Girl aged six.)

Living with a grandparent with Alzheimer's Disease

The clinical and pathological signs of Alzheimer's Disease were first researched by Alois Alzheimer in 1906. Alzheimer's Disease is recognised as the most common form of dementia in old age. According to research by Goate (1991) the number of people in the UK with Alzheimer's Disease was about 500,000. Graham (1991) estimates this figure will double by the end of the century. Buckman (1988) says 'living with uncertainty is painful in itself.' For many children and their parents there is little certainty about the future if a family member has Alzheimer's Disease. Children may be confused wondering what has happened to the person they used to know. Savishinsky (1990) says over half of carers of people with Alzheimer's Disease are troubled themselves by insomnia, depression and anxiety. This may be underpinned by opinion that there is a genetic base for the early onset of Alzheimer's Disease.

For the old person there is:

• a feeling of disorientation;
• an inability to grasp what is currently happening;
• hampered communication;
• changed personality.

Amy, aged seven, wrote this:

My Gran is not my Gran. She is called my Gran but that is all that is left. She lives in our house but most of the time her brain is not there any more. She isn't Dad's mum either. She asked him last week if he knew where her son was.

Disasters

The word 'disaster' is derived from the Latin 'astrum', or 'star', which may be translated as ill-starred or suffering misfortune. Generally disasters are thought to occur suddenly but they may also happen gradually and almost always the effects are long lasting before a process of recovery and normality. Parkes *et al.* (1996) describe disasters as 'traumatic losses involving ten or more deaths or extensive destruction'.

The media have a tendency to record disasters in terms of statistics which describe the numbers of people who have survived or perished. But for those involved, it is the pain and anguish which is central to the experience and, for survivors, the fact that life can never be the same again. Tragedies such as Hillsborough, Locherbie or Dunblane are sudden and they awaken an intensity of grief which can be overwhelming and extremely difficult to resolve.

At the centre of a trauma are the victims and the rescuers. Kinchin (1998), believes that when a person encounters a disaster 'the brain juggles between recalling the painfulness of the event (intrusion) and going to great lengths to forget it (avoidance)'. (p.44).

Erickson *et al.* (1976), describes disasters which strike individuals as 'a blow to the psyche that breaks through one's defences so suddenly and with such force that one cannot respond effectively'. Erickson describes mass disasters as 'blows to the tissues of social life that damage the bonds attaching people together'. (p. 110).

Disasters are commonly divided into two categories: man-made and natural. However, it is not unusual for both factors to combine, for example where a multiple road traffic accident occurs as a result of bad weather. Berren *et al.* (1982), describe five categories of disaster, according to the:

- degree of personal impact;
- type of disaster;
- potential for occurrence or reoccurrence;
- control over future impact;
- duration.

Other people, such as Tyhurst (1977), describe three overlapping phases in acute disasters.

- *The impact phase* when the event begins. In most cases this phase is quite short although in some cases it may be long-lived.

- *The recoil period* when the initial cause has ceased or people have escaped. During this period secondary stresses may occur.
- *The post-traumatic* period when both impact and recoil stresses are absent but individuals are subjected to the losses and the effects of the disaster in daily life.

An underlying philosophy which permeates much of the research on disasters is that generally catastrophies are survived, though they are seldom forgotten. Disasters, although overwhelmingly dreadful, also have a bizarre fascination attached to them. Years after horrifying events people still flock to the sites and every tragic detail is documented by the media.

The emotional cost of disasters

Humankind has learnt to respond to disasters both proactively and reactively and to develop sophisticated rescue and recovery services, yet as Raphael (1986) writes, 'One of the greatest human costs is the enormity of psychological experience...the scars on the mind', a view supported by Kinchin and Stewart (1998) and Hodgkinson (1991). These authors include rescue and support personnel amongst those who may be victims of emotional trauma following a disaster.

Post-traumatic stress disorder

Post-traumatic stress is defined by the World Health Organisation as the response which may follow an incident which is 'outside the range of usual human experience'. There are three categories of human response:
1. The experience reoccurs in thoughts, hallucinations, night terrors or flashbacks, so that the person concerned 'relives' the experience.
2. Situations which may evoke emotional responses associated with the event are avoided.
3. Sleep disorders, physical and emotional disturbances are common.

Reliving the event

Many children and young people will be troubled by flashbacks, sleep disturbances and intrusive thoughts. Although these may happen at any time, they are often instigated by an environment or an experience which reminds them of the trauma. These triggers are often sensory ones such as loud noises or smells.

After Stephanie had been rescued from the bedroom in her family's thatched cottage when a spark caught the roof alight, she became terrified of anything to do with fire or smoke. On one occasion when a friend burnt toast in food technology she ran out of the classroom screaming and shaking.

Avoiding situations and experiences which are reminders of what happened

Avoiding situations which trigger painful memories of bad experiences is a natural human response. Like adults, children soon learn to protect themselves from events which they anticipate will cause them emotional pain. In some cases this will also lead to the child avoiding people who may want to recall what happened. Conversely, children may avoid reminiscing because they do not wish to upset other people. Some young people will live for the present and avoid investing their hope in the future. Others will perhaps find comfort in religion.

Physical and emotional disturbances

Children and young people of all ages may experience heightened anxiety and arousal which manifests itself in:

- lack of concentration/poor memory;
- regression in academic performance or previously learnt skills;
- sleep disturbances;
- attachment difficulties/separation difficulties;
- phobias associated with situations akin to that of the disaster;
- exaggerated awareness of danger;
- irritability and aggression;
- anxiety and panic;
- depression;
- psychosomatic illness.

Kinchin (1998) is one of the most recent authors to have written extensively about post-traumatic stress disorder in children. He argues that as we approach the millennium, young people have a greater awareness of disasters than their ancestors did and that it is quite likely the number of children suffering from post-traumatic stress disorder is greater than the number of adults with the condition. Kinchin believes that children's illusions of safety have been steadily eroded over recent years.

Some characteristics of post-traumatic stress disorder which are unique to children are as follows:

- Repetitive (perhaps aggressive) play, containing themes about the traumatic event.
- Loss of recently acquired developmental skills.
- Omen-formation – a false belief in being able to predict future untoward events.
- Regressive behaviour, returning to thumb sucking, bed wetting, baby talk.
- Generalised fearfulness and separation anxiety.
- Not wanting to sleep alone, wanting to sleep with parents.
- Worrying about how parents have reacted to the trauma. (Kinchin 1998, p. 28.)

Mandy, a little girl with Down's Syndrome, was four when she witnessed her father being electrocuted and then run over by a high speed train. For three years afterwards she re-enacted the event in the home corner of her classroom and could not be persuaded by the teacher to look at pictures of trains. On the day of the school Christmas party another parent sent a cake into school in the shape of an engine. She swept it off the table with her arm signing 'Daddy train, Daddy train.'

The impact of a traumatic event depends on children's chronological age, cognitive understanding, degree to which they were involved, and the attachments which they have to the victims. There is some empirical evidence (Yule and Gold 1993) to suggest children from unstable home backgrounds (for example through the breaking down of family relationships, being a refugee, or victim of war) may endure the effects of trauma for longer than those in more supportive settings. Children of lower ability are also thought to be at greater risk.

Central to research concerning children and trauma has been the undeniable fact that children's responses are very like those of adults. For young children an anticipated disaster such as an earthquake or a hurricane is confusing. Whilst they are aware of the unrest of adults, they may also have a sense of excitement for, as yet, they have not learnt about danger. However, once the disaster strikes, children sense their parents' fear and are afraid of separation. If their parents are injured or in need of urgent care, children may be unable to comprehend what is happening. In extreme cases they may attempt to comfort adults.

During the post-impact or recoil phase, they may share an adult sense of relief that they have survived. However, as time goes on parental grief and unrest often impinges on children in the post-traumatic phase and they may feel acutely vulnerable, physically ill and suffer learning difficulties.

Where the death of a family member or carer has occurred, most children will have grief reactions, although in the very early years, as with any other bereavements, they may be unable to perceive the permanence of their loss. They will however identify with the responses of other siblings and adults and respond accordingly. The loss of material possessions such as the family home will also be traumatic.

Adolescents are more aware of the long-term consequences of death although, like adults, they may deny what has happened (Raphael 1986). Others may temper their reactions according to the expectations of their peer group or put their own grief aside in an attempt to support adults or younger siblings. Some may show anger or feel guilty that they were in some way to blame.

What do children need?
- Somebody with them whom they know.
- People who will listen patiently to what they have to say and how they choose to say it.

- Someone who will acknowledge what has happened.
- Someone who will allow them to express grief in any way they choose.
- People who will answer their questions openly and honestly.

Families and disasters

Families have particular significance in disaster. The way in which the members respond as a 'unit' has been the focus of several in-depth studies which reveal that some members may be more vulnerable than others (Bolin 1982, Trost and Hultaker 1983).

How families respond
- Survivors need to be together.
- Adults tend to be over-protective.
- There may be role changes.
- Closer bonding.

At the onset of the threat of an anticipated disaster, most families unite in an attempt to secure mutual protection and planned courses of action. The latter may include bringing relatives together to endure the trauma or, more frequently, attempting to evacuate next of kin outside the danger area. Where members are separated there is often considerable distress and even risking of life to achieve reunion.

At the time of impact, the family unit strives to avoid injury and death and to survive. Where this has not been possible, there is a period of desperate searching in the immediate post-disaster phase with young and most vulnerable people a priority. During the long-term recovery phase, there are social and cultural variations in response. However, in all cases, the emotional cost within victim families is persistent although family ties are generally strengthened (Bolin 1982). Bolin's study has also shown how family recovery is affected by material losses and relocation. Higher socio-economic classes have a tendency to do better and economic recovery seems to have the largest causal effect on emotional recovery. Elderly survivors appear to be particularly vulnerable, experiencing extreme difficulty in adjusting to relocation after the event.

Despite trauma, many families survive disasters and are more closely united units as a result. However, some do not, and amongst these are those where relationships were strained before the event.

Children are not immune from the physical or emotional trauma associated with tragedy and in the busy life of a school it can be easy to overlook the needs of young people. When children's needs are neglected it is rarely intentional. More often, adults are consumed in their own grief and they may be unable to grasp what is happening to children. The latter part of this book concerns itself with suggested school frameworks for both proactive and reactive responses to loss, change and grief in childrens' lives. Therefore an in-depth discussion of disaster management is not appropriate here. However, the following description by an experienced secondary school teacher demonstrates how in the face of adversity few educators feel equipped to cope.

> Up until then I had been fairly calm, almost operating on an automatic pilot. But as I ticked the names off my list, suddenly it hit me. How on earth could I tell Mr and Mrs Briggs that Sharon was dead? What about Mrs Harris who had relied on Gavin since his father died? Every name without a tick meant another set of parents to tell, another funeral to attend. I just knew I couldn't face that. I felt so helpless. (Quoted in Yule and Gold 1993, p. 11.)

Schools are not immune from tragedies either from within the school community, or the effects of circumstances outside.

Tragedies within the school community include:

- a fire, lightning strike or flood;
- the death through accident of a child, member of school staff or a member of a child's family;
- an act of violence such as murder or shooting;
- the death of a child, staff member or member of a child's family through serious illness.

Tragedies outside the school community include:

- serious accidents or deaths on school outings, residential trips;
- tragedies where large numbers of children die, for example the M40 minibus disaster (see Figure 5.2), Dunblane shooting;
- civil disturbances through violence, such as riots.

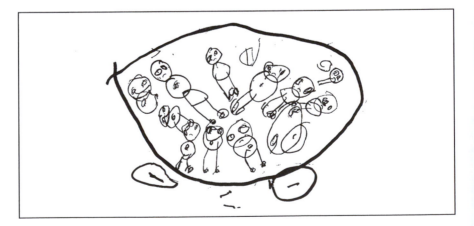

Figure 5.2 When the bus crashed they all fell down dead. Brother, aged three, of M40 minibus disaster victim

Chapter 6

The Caring Role of the School

Caring for children

The counsellor provides a non-judgmental, supportive relationship which enables individuals to enhance their self-esteem, self-respect and self-efficacy (confidence), in part by learning to search for their own answers and to rely on their own resources. Herbert (1996).

The words 'supportive-carer' may be more relevant for children than the term 'counsellor'. Through 'supporting' the adult listens to and communicates with the child in a purposeful way, which in turn enables the child to feel valued and respected. In this way the relationship is not a formal situation where a qualified counsellor receives the child as a 'client'. More importantly there is a relationship between the adult 'supporter' and the child which extends beyond boundaries and appointments.

Through the supportive care of an adult, children are helped to make sense of their life experiences. Sharing experiences helps to remove any feelings of isolation and to reduce their anxiety and fear. In other words, through the relationship which exists between the supportive adult and the child, the child is enabled to 'tell their story' in the knowledge that the adult will support them. The first contact between the supporter-carer and the child is very important and it will influence the success of the relationship. Children may be wondering:

- Can I talk to this adult?
- Will the adult listen to me?
- Will the adult think I am making a fuss about nothing?
- Can I trust this adult?

In this way the supportive-carer relationship is dependent on the attributes which the adult brings to the partnership and the way in which the adult is able to connect with the child and to perceive the child's experience. This relationship is founded on trust and should have a quality which helps the child to feel understood and safe enough to share very personal thoughts and experiences.

Teachers and professionals who are not trained counsellors can use counselling skills, responding to children's needs and concerns as they arise, so that the adult and the child explore what is happening together. Fundamental to the relationship between the child and the supportive-carer is the ability of the adult to use interpersonal skills such as listening, exploring, clarifying and responding. There are also situations where adults will require specialist skills if they are to work effectively with children who are experiencing clinical grief. These are not learnt overnight. They are professional capacities gained as the result of lengthy training which Parkes *et al.* (1996) describe as 'a theoretical basis of psychological and socio-functioning and a period of supervised practice'.

There are three fundamental components associated with the role of the supportive-carer:

- A capacity to convey to the child her uniqueness or worth.
- A capacity to perceive what the child may be experiencing and to convey this understanding sensitively.
- A capacity to convey genuine concern.

In many ways supporting children involves becoming more aware of the communication skills we use every day in the classroom. This includes our verbal language (or sign language) and our body language. The ability to communicate is an essential component of supporting children and listening is fundamental to all caring relationships. Communication includes understanding people's emotional responses and endeavouring to interpret whatever they are trying to tell us. Good communication involves total involvement with the child so that they are in no doubt that we are doing our very best to understand how it might be to be in their shoes.

As educators we strive to improve our schools, our working environments, and the potential for children's learning progress. But supporting children is not just about 'doing' – it is about 'being' present and in touch with the child at their point of need. However, when we are perceptive enough to determine the child's point of need, this can cause us to reflect on our own vulnerability; and unless we are in touch with our own feelings, the child's experiences may trigger our own responses and catch us unaware. We may then fall into the trap of concentrating on our own thoughts rather than on the child we are supporting.

Naming feelings communicates our empathy with the child and also helps her to understand that we are in touch with what she is experiencing. Emotions are, however, very personal. There are levels of feelings within a person which we can never fully determine from the outside. This should not prevent us from endeavouring to communicate empathetic understanding. But it is a challenge, particularly if the child is not able to communicate verbally or to answer our questions.

Checking the quality of the supportive-carer relationship

To help us reflect on our interactions with children it may be helpful to ask ourselves the following questions:

- Does the child perceive me as giving her my full attention?
- How do I convey my empathy and understanding to the child?
- What does my verbal and non-verbal language convey to the child?
- Are my questions open-ended, inviting the child to tell her story?

Confidentiality and the supportive-carer relationship

We all set limits in our relationships and each of us has boundaries which preserve our own identities as individuals. But the strength of the boundary depends on the nature and context of the relationship. In the supportive-carer relationship between a child and an adult, the adult strives to create a safe environment where the child feels sufficiently comfortable and valued to share her experiences and concerns. For this to happen it is essential that there is trust and confidentiality, but inevitably there will be times when the capacity of the adult to support the child fully will entail sharing information with other people. Therefore it is very important to agree with the child at the beginning of the relationship that in order to support him fully, other people may need to be involved.

All schools will have policies which relate to Child Protection and teachers should be clear how to respond if a child shares personal information or something comes to their attention which may effect either their short-term or their long-term welfare.

What reassurance can we give children?
- Reassure them you will not reveal information carelessly or unnecessarily.
- Reassure them that any information they share will only be discussed with people who need to know and that other people will treat it confidentially.
- Reassure them their welfare is of prime importance.
- Reassure them that if it is necessary to share information with other people you will ask the child's permission to do this.

The role of the supportive-carer when a child and its family are suffering grief after a death

Children and their families will need different support during the phases of their grief. There are two main phases:

Phase 1 or the impact phase

This phase lasts from the time of the death, through the funeral and for about two or three months afterwards. It is important that children and their families are familiar with people who will support them at this time of crisis. In many cases this will include extended family members and people such as GPs. The events surrounding the death will still be very new and everyone will be struggling to come to terms with what has happened. The overriding concern will be to prevent further distress.

Phase 2 or the adjustment phase

After the shock of the death and the funeral is over and the pace of life has returned to 'normal', many adults and children will begin to experience grief. The role of the supportive-carer is to:

- Establish a relationship.
- Support the child through the pain of loss, change and grief and to convey sensitive understanding of the child's needs.
- Help the child to identify and express feelings and to be in touch with their own emotions.
- Provide continuing and reliable support.

Supporting bereaved children and their families uses many of the professional capacities outlined earlier in the book. Central to the role is the trusting relationship which develops between the supportive-carer and those she is helping. Different kinds of grief have also been described in earlier chapters. Worden's (1988) tasks of grieving provide a framework for support.

Children and their families will need opportunities which help them to:

- Accept the reality of the loss.
- Work through the pain of their grief.
- Adjust to life without the person who has died.
- Retain the aspects of the relationship which were important, for example drawing on positive memories.
- Reach a healthy resolution to their grief.

Using counselling and communication skills

When children are unhappy and grieving they often find it hard to concentrate which may mean that in conversations which they have with us they are darting around from one subject to another. Although this may be helpful to the child, because it gives them autonomy to choose what they say, it can be very difficult for adults to gain a clear picture of what is happening. Taking time during the conversation to summarise what the child has said so far may have two helpful outcomes. Firstly, it helps the child to know that what they have said is important and secondly, it helps the adult to check that they have understood correctly. Summarising does not, however, mean just a mechanical repetition of what has been said. It means finding our own words to reflect back to the child what they have said, both in content and in the emotions they have expressed.

Having feelings understood can be very affirming. In order to be fully in touch with how children express emotions we need to listen very carefully to what they say and how their levels of emotional response are articulated through different words. There will be times when children who are usually verbally articulate will be at a loss for words. This is especially so when they are struggling with painful feelings. Silence may seem prolonged and uncomfortable for the adult but generally it is not like this for the child. Space for thought may give them an opportunity to reflect on what is happening to them and to communicate this in a different way, for example through their body language or play.

There is a special quality about reflective silence which embraces an acceptance and understanding. Therefore it is important not to interrupt too soon. The child may be supported non-verbally through gesture or perhaps through holding their hand. There will also be occasions when empathetic listening will involve talking to the child about what we suspect is troubling them, enabling them to explore their own thoughts and experiences. Direct and indirect questions may also be helpful.

Direct or closed questions

When we use a direct question we expect to receive a factual answer. So if we ask a child, 'Did you go to visit your Gran's grave at the weekend?' we invite the child to provide us with information around a specific focus without encouraging them to give us more information than we have asked for.

Indirect or open questions

Indirect questions give much more opportunity for a child to choose how he replies. They invite the child to engage in a conversation with us. So if we ask the child 'What did you do at the weekend?' it invites him to tell us as much as he wishes about his weekend. Sometimes children do not know what they are feeling because their emotions overlap. There may be, for instance, angry feelings surrounding sadness. Sensing these differences is sometimes called 'empathy at the edge of awareness' (Mearns and Thorne 1988). As adults we tiptoe with great care because children may either consciously or unconsciously hide these feelings because they are afraid.

What does the child need?
- A supportive-carer who conveys empathy.
- A supportive-carer who is non-judgmental and does not show a shocked reaction to anything shared.

- A supportive-carer who allows them to express their emotions.
- A supportive-carer who checks they understand what has been communicated.
- A supportive-carer who uses open-ended questions.
- A supportive-carer who helps them to make sense of their experiences.
- A supportive-carer whom they can trust.
- A supportive-carer who offers a safe environment.

Being professional will necessitate supportive-carers having a capacity to be emotionally detached from children without appearing to be uncaring and remote. Geldard and Geldard (1997) refer to this as an ability to be 'a calm and stable facilitator, who is able to participate when necessary, and always to listen, accept and understand the child.' (p. 17). Figure 6.1 shows the elements of a good relationship between the teacher as supportive-carer and the child.

Caring for colleagues and ourselves

In the aftermath of tragedies such as Omagh and Hillsborough the need to 'care for the carers' and 'counsel the counsellors' has been highlighted. For teachers, caring extends beyond the individual child who is grieving. The child is part of a birth family or care family and a member of the school family, so in reaching out to the child, we may also find ourselves caring for the needs of the parents, the child's peer group, the family, colleagues and ourselves. Although not all families need professional intervention, many will welcome support. Teachers have a responsibility to reach out to these families and to communicate their willingness to become involved.

The vulnerability of the supportive-carer

Many teachers and professionals suffer from personal stress as a result of a commitment to caring for somebody else. Often this effects the carer's personal life. Therefore peer support is very important, especially within a school, since carers need opportunities to interact with people in equal two-way relationships.

Caring will involve:

- an awareness of how colleagues may respond to stress;
- willingness to offer personal and professional support;
- acknowledging the stress colleagues are under;
- encouraging colleagues to seek specialist professional support if necessary.

Several studies are focused on the stress experienced by people caring for children and their families (Landsdown and Goldman 1988, Faulkner *et al.* 1995). Although this research has concentrated on how professionals cope

A capacity to convey the child's uniqueness and worth	A capacity to convey an understanding of the child's experience	A capacity to convey genuineness
The supportive carer will demonstrate this through:	**The supportive carer will demonstrate this through:**	**The supportive carer will demonstrate this through:**
• giving the child time • giving the child undivided attention • not interrupting when they are talking • allowing the child to express their feelings in any way they wish, as long as they do not endanger themselves or anyone else • knowing the child and his/her home background well • helping the child to have some control over what is happening.	• helping the child to feel safe • showing empathy • being sensitive to how the child feels and responds and communicating this to the child • showing a capacity to enter into the child's world • checking own assumptions do not disagree with what the child has communicated.	• making sure communication and body language are congruent with what is said • responding naturally • being spontaneous • talking <u>appropriately</u> about own experience, helping the child to feel less isolated

Figure 6.1 Components of a trusting relationship between the supportive-carer and the child

with children who are life-limited, the findings seem to be relevant to teachers concerned with loss, change and grief in children's lives more generally.

In a study by Brown (1993) teachers from five primary schools cited the following factors as contributing to their stress:

- Witnessing pain and distress experienced by families.
- Feeling unskilled in dealing with emotional responses.
- Physical exhaustion as a result of emotional trauma.
- Poor communication between themselves and families or other carers.

These same teachers were aware that coping strategies which they found helpful to themselves might have an adverse effect on the children and their families that they were caring for. Strategies included distancing themselves from the child; guarding against involvement with the child; sharing concerns with colleagues; sharing concerns with their own families at home; finding opportunities to improve their professional skills. For families and children, the first two strategies adopted do not provide a solution, although the teachers had intended to rectify this through seeking support for themselves in order to sustain them in their caring role. There is frequently a tension between personal needs and professional expectations. In every human interaction there is a right distance which will be determined by the relationship. When we are working in schools our relationships contribute to the well-being of the school family. The balance between becoming over-involved with people or professionally detached is a difficult one. The latter can lead to a lack of meaningful communication; the former to attachments which may be inappropriate in school and be difficult to relinquish. Support is essential if teachers are to cope with difficulties and minimise professional stress. Indeed, without support their capacities will be diminished and their confidence undermined.

Dyregrov (1991) believes the stress experienced by adults working with grieving children may be greater than that of adults supporting other adults. 'We identify more with a child, more easily make their grief our own, and find it more difficult to stop thinking about what has happened, (p. 111). In other words, children's vulnerability potentially has the effect of awakening our own vulnerability and in turn leading to what Geldard and Geldard (1997) call 'emotional depletion'. Figure 6.2 shows ways in which the carer's well-being can be safeguarded.

Caring for each other

In good schools, people have time for each other amidst the hustle and bustle of activity. Teachers are used to creating support networks for their pupils. Nevertheless some people are more comfortable supporting colleagues than others. Sharing responsibilities with colleagues provides an opportunity for continuity of care as well as protection from stress and burn out. Team relationships are important. In many ways they involve the same principles as

When the carer is able to seek **SUPPORT**	this can result in →	• less stress • a safeguard against isolation • affirming skills • an affirmation of endeavours
When the carer is able to seek **CLARIFICATION**	this can result in →	• reinforcing personal and professional capacities • a safeguard against over-involvement
When the carer has opportunities for **EVALUATION**	this can result in →	• a realistic assessment of whether objectives are being met • an opportunity to assess stress or 'burn-out' • opportunities for personal growth
When the carer has opportunities for **CONSULTATION**	this can result in →	• opportunities to match the support available with the individual needs of children and families

Figure 6.2 Safeguarding the carer

working with children and their families. However it can be difficult to determine the needs of individuals within the caring ethos of the school. Parkes *et al.* (1996) make an interesting differentiation between wants and needs. They also describe how a person will sometimes want something which is not in their best interest or need.

There are two fundamental capacities associated with the role of caring for others – effective communication and an awareness and interest in interacting with other people. Where carers are successfully supported by other people their needs are respected. This respect will be affirmed through:

• Helping each other to feel at ease.
• Creating an atmosphere which is relaxed yet purposeful.
• Giving each other individual attention.
• Safeguarding against distractions when we are attending to others' needs.
• Contributing helpful resources.

Caring for ourselves

Counsellors are well known for their inability to negotiate their own help and support systems. Murgatroyd and Woolfe (1993) stress the importance of recognising our own limitations which enhances the likelihood of giving appropriate help in a professional capacity, so that neither the carer nor the person who is being helped feel compromised. She goes on to explain that experiencing emotional responses such as powerlessness and inadequacy go hand in hand with grief. They are not indicators of failure or non-professional behaviour. They are human responses. Caring unconditionally for other people and giving them individual attention are attributes often associated with carers. However these capacities may conflict strongly with feelings which may be experienced during periods of stress.

The relationship which exists between ourselves and a child or his or her family is often an unbalanced one where we do most of the giving and the child and the family do a large proportion of the receiving. It is important that we are able to recognise our own emotional depletion. This will include:

- Feeling overworked and unable to delegate.
- Feeling physically exhausted and ineffective.
- Feeling hopeless and helpless.
- Low motivation.
- Physical illness and vulnerability to infection.
- Negative attitudes towards other people.
- Gaining little job satisfaction.

Our willingness to support families should not undermine our own needs.

Recognising our own grief and our own mortality

Caring for others is emotionally demanding, especially in the emotive environment of loss and grief. We all bring our past experiences (including loss and grief) to the present. They are an intrinsic part of what shapes our humanity. As Simos (1979) writes: 'treatment of the bereaved needs to emerge from a compassion based on recognition of the common vulnerability of all human beings in the face of loss' (p. 177). Worden (1988) cautiously reminds carers that although their past experiences of loss and grief may help them to develop an empathetic relationship with the client, unresolved losses may also hinder the partnership. Indeed Geldard and Geldard (1997) caution that 'being empathetic can be hazardous to a counsellor's study'. This potential inhibition may include losses which are feared by the carer as well as those which have been experienced. Although these losses do not generally create acute apprehension, they may still create a state of mind which interferes with the effective supportive-carer role. Supportive-carers often find themselves affected in several ways:

- by the grief of the family;
- by the memories of their own losses;
- by fears for the future.

A heightened awareness of our own personal mortality may also be the result of working with other people who are experiencing loss and grief. At other times carers may find themselves identifying with the person they are supporting. To safeguard against burdening children and families with our own losses we should:

- Identify conflict or unresolved losses in our own lives.
- Face past losses honestly and squarely.
- Identify personal limitations in our own capacity to support others.
- Be aware of our own attachment to the client.
- Share responsibilities with colleagues.
- Be familiar with sources of specialist support. (See resource section at the end of the book.)

Chapter 7

Exploring Loss, Change and Death in the School Curriculum

Children today are in a strange situation. Witnessing death in their own families and communities has largely been banished and adults speak about the end of life in euphemisms and metaphors. Stories have 'tidy', happy endings. At the same time the media provides young people with a multitude of images of death and destruction which portray other people's experiences.

An exploration of death combines mysterious and imaginative concepts with those which are physical and practical. Piaget (1951) claimed that children's curiosity only began with cognisance of death. But my own experience tells me that very young children are aware of the responses of adults to grief and they make connections between the nature of death and their own mortality. Most teachers of children in the early years will have been presented with the body of a dead insect or other creature by a curious child. Recently Becky, aged five, told me, 'You see that big tree – the one in the corner – that's where we put the birds and the squirrels and the hamster and the frog and all the others in their boxes when they are *deaded*.'

Older children are challenging and far-reaching in their attempts to answer ultimate questions about life and death and the practicalities about death and dying. Ben, aged 13, questioned, 'How do they drain the blood out of people when they embalm them?' His friend remarked during a PSE lesson, 'Unless you can explain why a good God can kill my baby sister when she is asleep, I'll never believe in religion again.'

In a biological sense there is nothing particularly mysterious about death. Death is a natural conclusion to the end of life. But while it may be within the natural order of things, the grief which it brings should not be trivialised. To deny children opportunities to understand about death and to explore their own feelings is to sell them short. It certainly does not fulfil the expectations of the Education Reform Act (1988) which states that the central aim of the school curriculum is to promote the: 'spiritual, moral, cultural, mental and physical development of pupils and of society, and prepare pupils for the opportunities, responsibilities and experiences of adult life.'

Gatliffe (1988) feels children should be prepared for the 'reality of death' through 'death education' and this can best be done through the framework for Religious Studies or Religious Education although she does not deny the topic could also be approached in subjects such as biology and science. Indeed the

National Curriculum Orders for Science (1994) include: life processes in plants, animals and humans in the Programmes of Study at Key Stages 1–3.

A large number of LEA Agreed Syllabuses for Religious Education published since the 1988 Education Reform Act include aspects of death and mourning in their Programmes of Study. Rotherham Metropolitan Borough Council Agreed Syllabus (1989), states: 'Topics in which Religious Education may be the central purpose include new life; ageing and death; beginnings and endings; growth; change; suffering.' The Oldham Agreed Syllabus (1990) lists under learning experiences at Key Stage 2: 'To ask and explore questions relating to identity and the human condition e.g. life, death and suffering.'

In 1993, the Minister of State for Education asked the National Curriculum Council (NCC), and subsequently the School Curriculum and Assessment Authority (SCAA), to produce Model Syllabuses for Religious Education. Faith communities and teachers were extensively involved in this task and two models were developed. Model 1 is structured around a knowledge and understanding of what it means to be a member of a faith community. Model 2 is concerned with a knowledge and understanding of the teachings of religions and how these relate to shared human experience. Included in Model 1 'Learning Experiences for pupils at Key Stage 2 (Judaism) it is suggested pupils could: 'Find out about Jewish customs connected with birth and death and discuss their thoughts and feelings about death.' At the same Key Stage pupils who are studying Sikhism could: 'Talk about their own feelings about death and whether there is an afterlife.'

Although the Model Syllabuses are not statutory documents they are intended for use by Agreed Syllabus Conferences in the preparation of new syllabuses. Therefore most statutory LEA documents follow the guidance of the SCAA syllabuses.

The Hertfordshire Agreed Syllabus (1995) advocates that pupils should:

• Develop awareness of the fundamental questions of life arising from human experiences through responses to awe, wonder, sorrow, death of pets etc.
• Be given opportunities to develop their sense of enquiry and curiosity about life, death and relationships.

Death in the classroom

The remainder of this chapter describes the findings of a two year small-scale research project. Phase 1 set out to explore teacher awareness of loss, change and grief in the lives of the pupils they taught. It also sought to determine how the Programmes of Study concerning death and dying in County Agreed Syllabuses and Diocesan Syllabuses for Religious Education were being taught in schools. Phase 2 of the study evaluated the impact of in-service training sessions on the theme of loss, change and grief in children's lives and suggested a framework for individual schools planning a Scheme of Work in Religious Education at Key Stages 1–3. Emphasis was placed on children's understanding of, and response to, death in both phases of the research.

Phase 1

Twenty primary schools and ten middle schools from a variety of rural, city and urban settings in London and the Home Counties were selected as the focus for the research. Of these schools, over a third were church-controlled or church-aided. Pupils came from a variety of religious, cultural and home backgrounds.

The participants in the research were class teachers who responded to an invitation from their LEA or their Diocese to take part. Some participants had very clear reasons for wanting to invest a considerable amount of time and effort in the project:

> We have to fit the needs of the grieving child into the busy rigour of the school day. I need to be shown how to do this, but I think it is a matter for the whole school, rather than my problem alone.

> I want something which will help me feel confident talking to children about death.

Others sought a balance between enhancing their teaching skills and developing greater sensitivity in order to help children as they grew up.

> The things which children need are probably the same whatever the circumstances of the loss. As a teacher, I want to be able to give children information so that they can make sense of what has happened. I want to be able to give them reassurance and to know what they are likely to feel in the years ahead.

Two methods of data collection were used, namely questionnaires and interviews. The findings for Phase 1 are summarised under four main headings:

- Loss, change and death as appropriate topics for primary and middle school pupils.
- Children's experience of loss, change and death.
- How teachers cope when they are faced with a grieving child.
- How children express their grief.

Loss, change and death as appropriate topics for primary and middle school pupils

At the onset of the research there was an awareness of death as a 'taboo' subject.

> Some parents view learning about loss and change in the same way as they view sex education. In other words, they are quite happy the subject is being taught in school as long as their child does not go home and ask questions and they do not know the answers.

Although 90 per cent of participants agreed it was appropriate to include the topics in the taught school curriculum, only a small minority of the teachers were aware that their County or Diocesan syllabus required them to teach about death and dying within the Programmes of Study at Key Stages 1–3. Where schools had attempted to teach about the topic, this had largely been at Key Stages 2–3 although themes such as emotions, growth and beginnings were very popular in Reception and Year 1–2 classes. City schools made reference to the depth and range of knowledge required when working with children from religious and cultural backgrounds. One teacher commented:

> Although I am totally committed to teaching, some of the kids get me very confused about what I should be teaching them about life after death. It strikes me that nobody really has the answer anyway because none of us have died. Yet children still ask, 'What is heaven like Sir?', and before you know where you are other children have joined in the conversation and they start arguing about it.

Generally there was an awareness that children would also bring experiences to school which needed to be addressed pastorally. In nearly all cases teachers gave anecdotal evidence of this:

> Because I have the Reception class, every single child I teach is experiencing a change in environment and a loss of familiar people when they arrive.

> At the beginning of the term I had six children without one parent at home. All of these children are bereft. Even a child whose father has gone to prison because he has been abusing him, longs for life to be what it was when the family were all together.

A large proportion of teachers felt they needed to acquire basic counselling skills if they were to support children.

Children's experience of loss, change and death

Ninety per cent of schools were able to identify recent experiences of loss, change and death in children's lives. The breakdown of family relationships was the most frequently cited cause.

> He suddenly got landed with new step siblings in his life whom he neither accepted nor wanted. He became angry with both his mother and her partner and spoke of his rage using furious adjectives.

Urban communities had the highest incidence of grief associated with social factors such as violence or the imprisonment of a family member.

> I have a brother and sister in my class. Their mother went away for the weekend and never came home. She has left them and their Dad to go and

live with someone else. The children's father is violent so they are both in care. The only time they see anyone they know is at Christmas when they get a visit from their grandparents.

Two of the children have a father in prison. They know their Dad is in gaol but it doesn't stop them thinking he will come home. Their Mum says they fight over who will sit in his chair at breakfast and at supper.

City schools also referred to refugee children and to those in temporary housing or bed and breakfast accommodation encountering change and loss. Those from ethnic minorities were often described as having poor language skills which hampered their ability to communicate how they felt.

Jitendra came to us as a refugee. He hardly ever spoke about his parents or the rest of his family. It was as if he felt guilty they had been left behind and he was the one who had been given the chance.

Only two schools were unable to give examples of children having suffered bereavement through the death of a family member or close friend during the previous year. Some schools had pupils who had witnessed or had been closely involved with death through tragic accidents.

In our village we had a case of drowning. Three of the children were playing on the ice one weekend when it broke and one boy fell in. He went under and was drowned. The whole community has been stunned by what happened but nobody has really talked to the children about how they feel. All they have done is give them the safety warnings about keeping away from the water.

I have a little girl of six in my class. She came to school in the morning and all was well. By lunchtime her Daddy had been killed and her life had changed for ever.

Nearly a quarter of school communities had been bereaved during the year before the onset of the research project. Most commonly this had been through the death of a member of staff or someone closely associated with the school. A head teacher in an infant school commented, 'Nobody tells you about things like this when you sign up to be a teacher.' Figure 7.1 shows the relative frequencies of the various causes of loss, change and grief.

How teachers cope when they are faced with a grieving child

Over half of the teachers felt ill-equipped to cope when a child suffered grief, although nearly all of these said they had made an attempt to support the child through 'empathy' and 'listening'. This had not always been successful because of timetable constraints, especially in the middle schools. Nearly all of the adults

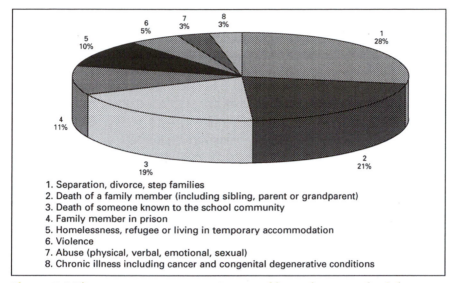

1. Separation, divorce, step families
2. Death of a family member (including sibling, parent or grandparent)
3. Death of someone known to the school community
4. Family member in prison
5. Homelessness, refugee or living in temporary accommodation
6. Violence
7. Abuse (physical, verbal, emotional, sexual)
8. Chronic illness including cancer and congenital degenerative conditions

Figure 7.1 The most common experiences of loss, change and grief reported by teachers in the 30 schools studied

interviewed needed to share their feelings about children with colleagues and some of these relied on school staff to support them, particularly when an event in a child's life triggered their own emotional responses. Others tried to cope alone: 'At the time I coped really well but when I got in the car at the end of the day, I just howled. It was as if the bits inside of me which hurt had been wounded again.'

Most were reluctant to discuss their own grief at home. A female teacher said: 'If you have to take your classroom into your sitting room, your families soon get fed up with that.'

Several people had sought professional guidance outside school but without exception they would have preferred to have been supported by their school community.

Where pupils from a school had died, generally the class teacher had attended the funeral and made an effort to keep in touch with the family afterwards. Sometimes other members of staff had also attended the funeral but more commonly they had visited graves or gardens of remembrance.

A major source of teachers' anxiety was a lack of knowledge concerning details of ceremonies of death and mourning in world religions. How teachers heard news seemed to play an important role in their capacity to support children. Most were told through a phone message to school passed on by the head teacher. There were several situations where teachers had been given information by families but had been asked to withhold it from children. On other occasions children had written about an event or divulged information to a class group or to a teacher without warning. A male teacher had learned about the death of a child's father in the local press. He described his response as: 'I wish I had heard some other way. It seemed so detached and sterile. Now I understand about Mark's behaviour, but I find it very difficult to grasp that in this day and age I had to find out like this.'

Another female teacher had heard bad news 'via the grapevine'.

How children express their grief

Teachers were unanimous in their view that children suffer grief as a result of loss, change and death. There were many descriptions of grief responses but it was extremely difficult to determine from questionnaires exactly how children expressed their feelings. The most common categories of response seemed to fall within the broad descriptors of anxiety, changed behaviour and regression in academic progress. It was interesting that in nearly three quarters of the interviews, teachers attempted to describe the intensity of the emotional response. Words such as 'extremely', 'very', 'a bit' were used.

Children's anxiety was described as:

- worry
- fear
- tension
- unhappiness
- unsettled.

Children's behaviour was described as:

- swings of mood
- unpredictable
- irritable
- out of character
- inability to concentrate
- withdrawn
- distant
- aggressive
- unable to communicate
- truancy
- lying
- stealing.

Changes in academic progress were described as:

- regression to a previous level
- loss of skills
- reluctance to communicate.

Some teachers seemed to suggest the younger the child, the more readily sadness was expressed. Similarly teachers' comments reflect a tendency in adolescents to react more aggressively, although there were several instances when teachers across Key Stages 1–3 reported that children hardly showed any reaction at all.

Information concerning the type of language which children used to talk about the breakdown of family relationships included the phrases 'gone away', 'not there any more'. Often these phrases seemed to be used to describe what the child perceived to be an impermanent situation, believing the absent person might return. There were also anecdotal descriptions of children who seemed to feel they might possess magical power which could reverse the process of death: 'Rachel knew the fish was dead but she kept returning to the fish tank asking, "Why can't he swim off now?" and, "If I tickle his back will he swim away?"'

At Key Stage 3 most young people used the term 'dead' or 'died' to describe death, together with detailed factual information about the event. Younger children spoke of people 'going to heaven' or 'away' when referring to someone who had died. After death the person was often described as being 'an angel' or 'a star'. Children from faith backgrounds who spoke about death usually used language which reflected their family religious belief and practice. Muhammad, aged seven, wrote:

> When my grandad died, the angels asked him all the good and all the bad. If it is good it will be OK but if it is bad, it is bad. I will not die for ever. Something will happen and I will sit up again. My grandad did that.

Although verbal language was often used by children they also expressed their feelings and recounted their experiences to their teachers in other ways.

> Often it isn't just the words which they say but the body language they display and the role-play they use which helps you understand there are things which are important in other cultures. I had a Hindu child in my class who told me her Granny was cremated in her wedding sari. She chose a piece of red fabric from the collage box and laid it on top of a table saying, 'Dadi Maa gone, Dadi Maa gone'.

Where children asked questions, they often required factual information, especially what happened to a body after death. Other questions arose in peer group discussions. For example: 'I think when people die they either go down or up. Down is bad. Why doesn't Parvin believe in the downstairs?'

It could be concluded the grief reactions of children are varied and individual. A school with a small number of pupils with special educational needs described the responses of two Year 2 children as: 'Curling up in a corner in a foetal position, rocking gently backwards and forwards' or, 'clutching to the bag she carried like it was her last chance of remaining in touch with something familiar'.

Phase 2

Phase 2 of the project built on the findings of Phase 1. Schools were encouraged to create a school policy statement for including the topic of loss, change and death within the Programmes of Study outlined in their LEA or Diocesan syllabus for Religious Education. None of the schools had previously considered a policy framework although all the teachers involved were unanimous in their view that grief and bereavement were part of their children's life experiences. Most of the teachers had been reluctant to tackle the subjects previously because they had not felt confident in their ability to do so.

All teachers attended three days of in-service training to develop their awareness of children's responses to loss and change and to increase their own knowledge of religious beliefs and practices concerning death and dying, before the onset of Phase 2. In addition, it was emphasised that each school would be expected to enter into a period of preparation and consultation before writing and drafting a policy or attempting to plan a Scheme of Work. Each teacher involved in the project attended a meeting where the management and monitoring of school policies was explained and a suggested plan of action was given, together with the relevant section from the LEA or Diocesan syllabus for Religious Education.

School policy statements

Each school prepared a short policy statement for teaching about loss, change and death. Each policy had six broad headings:

- Rationale for including teaching about loss, change and death in the curriculum.
- The objectives of the curriculum framework, taking into account the LEA or Diocesan syllabus.
- Consultation and discussion in the school.
- Phase(s) of education to be included in the curriculum.
- Curriculum breadth and content.
- Review and development of the policy.

Rationale for including aspects of loss, change and death in the school curriculum

Most of the schools described helping children learn about and come to terms with loss, change and death as part of a 'balanced and broadly-based curriculum'. All schools acknowledged the large proportion of their pupils who might be experiencing loss, change or grief at any one time. Some also referred to 'preparing pupils for the opportunities and experiences of adult life'. Others quoted their LEA or Diocesan syllabus Programme of Study.

Objectives for teaching about loss, change and death

Each school was asked to list up to six objectives for teaching about loss, change and death. An analysis of these revealed that many related to the stated ethos of the schools concerned or to the pastoral curriculum. The need for inner city schools to teach about faith and cultural beliefs and practices was evident. Generally the objectives showed a fair balance between the development of concepts, knowledge, attitudes and skills and issues which related to the pastoral needs of children, families and staff. Not surprisingly they also related to the stated objectives of the Religious Education syllabuses, including the development of children's capacities, skills and knowledge.

The objectives of one rural primary school read:

- To help children understand human experience of loss, change and death.
- To support children and their families when sad things happen.
- To help children to develop capacities and skills so that, as prospective parents, they do not regard death as a taboo subject.
- To help children develop concepts about loss, change and death.
- To help children to understand how different people respond to death and what they believe happens to the spirit of the person after death.

An inner-city middle school stated the following objectives:

- To develop a school awareness of children's everyday experience of loss, change and death.
- To help children to grow up without feeling death is a 'taboo' subject.
- To help pupils to express and explore their feelings so that they are able to put themselves in the shoes of other people.
- To help pupils understand the beliefs and practices associated with death and dying.
- To help parents and the wider community to accept that educating children about loss and change means educating them about life experiences.
- To combat ignorance and nurture understanding amongst faith and cultural communities.

Consultation and discussion in schools

It was emphasised that for a policy and a curriculum to be implemented successfully, teachers needed to liaise closely with everyone concerned with the children's education. Individual teachers worked with members of their school senior management team and Governors and agreed a rationale for the objectives of the school policy. Several primary and middle feeder schools also included staff from schools where their pupils would go when they left their current phase of education. Others welcomed support staff and parents to their meetings. An innovative teacher in a middle school interviewed Year 6 pupils to ascertain whether the children thought death was a good subject to learn about. One child had said: 'It looks really interesting finding out about graves and things.' Another had commented: 'When my cat died nobody talked about it. I was sad about that. It would have been good if my friends had been able to help me but they didn't know what to say. These lessons might help somebody else.'

Over three-quarters of the schools discussed their objectives with parents at

PTA meetings and all of these schools intended to include a statement in their school prospectus when a new edition was published. A minority of 12 per cent of schools consulted members of their local faith communities. Mostly this was to secure information about death rites and funerals.

During Phase 1, I had selected six possible areas for teaching about loss, change and death from LEA and Diocesan syllabuses for Religious Education and asked teachers to list suitable content to be taught across Key Stages 1–3. It was emphasised that all areas might not be relevant at each Key Stage. The aim was to endeavour to show continuity and progression in content.

The six content areas

The areas selected were as follows:

- Drawing on individual pupils' experience of loss, change and death.
- Exploring loss, change and death in language, literature and the arts.
- Exploring children's questions and concerns.
- Teaching about customs, rituals and practices associated with death and dying in world faiths.
- Teaching about the beliefs of faith communities concerning what happens at the time of death and beyond.
- Cultural and organisational aspects of death and dying.

The content of individual school curriculum frameworks closely reflected the six areas above and largely matched the LEA or Diocesan syllabus.

Drawing on pupils' experience of loss, change and death

All schools included drawing on pupils' experiences of loss, change and death in their Programmes of Study, and some schools also included reference to children's questions and concerns under this heading. The natural world; new siblings; growth; war; violence; separation and divorce, were among topics listed. Only four schools did not list emotional responses. Interestingly including emotional responses was largely limited to Key Stages 1–2. Reference to national and world issues was largely confined to Key Stage 3.

More than three-quarters of the schools included transition to another school. Homelessness and unemployment featured more often in inner-city schools.

Exploring loss, change and death in language, literature and the arts

Many of the LEA or Diocesan syllabuses made direct reference to the use of language, story or literature in their Programmes of Study. Some syllabuses mentioned the arts and children's own writing as valuable resources for the exploration and expression of feelings. At Key Stage 1 most teachers seemed to rely heavily on picture and story books as resources. At Key Stages 2–3 schools suggested developing the topic through reference to architecture, music, poetry and art. A detailed list of books is included at the end of this book.

Exploring children's own questions and concerns

Although all LEA and Diocesan syllabuses include this dimension in their Programmes of Study, e.g. 'to consider and to ask ultimate questions' (Hounslow) or, 'Most or all general topics can raise questions about the nature and meaning of life' (Berkshire), teachers rarely offered examples of what might be included. The exception was a Hillingdon school which listed questions within Key Stage 3 as: 'Can things or animals come back to life?', 'What happens when a person dies?' What is a dead body like?', 'How long can I expect to live?'

Teaching about customs, rituals and practices associated with death and dying in world faiths.

The questionnaire responses indicated that this was one of the priority curriculum areas. Therefore it is hardly surprising to find teachers suggesting a wide range of topics and themes, especially since a whole day of in-service training had been devoted to death in world religions. Most of the content was based on Programmes of Study from the LEA or Diocesan syllabuses which included family gatherings and shared meals at Key Stage 1 and signs, symbols and artefacts at Key Stages 2–3. Within Key Stage 3, more than half the schools thought pupils should be given opportunities to develop an understanding of the significance which ceremonies associated with death and dying have for believers.

Teaching about the beliefs of faith communities concerning what happens at the time of death and beyond

Most schools quoted directly from their LEA or diocesan syllabus under this heading but failed to suggest the activities which might be included. Themes of 'remembrance', and 'saying thank you for peoples' lives' were popular at Key Stage 1. Understandably teachers were reluctant to commit themselves in an area where they had already expressed concern about their lack of knowledge.

Cultural and organisational aspects of death and dying

Like the previous area of content, few schools offered their own suggestions although there were examples from history and geography Schemes of Work. One middle school suggested pupils could:

Key Stage 1

- Consider how life experiences and milestones are marked.
- Explore local burial places.

Key Stage 2

- Visit museums.
- Visit places of worship.

Key Stage 3

- Find out information about how to record a death.
- Explore attitudes to death, past and present.
- Find out about local places in the community eg. places of rest; mortuary; crematorium.

All the schools were ready to introduce aspects of loss, change and death within the RE curriculum during the last term of the research project. Figure 7.2 shows a framework for these themes across Key Stages 1, 2 and 3. Teachers were asked to plan no more than four lessons which might take place over a period of half a term. I made a visit to each of the schools and interviewed one of the teachers who had introduced loss, change and death into the Scheme of Work for Religious Education. The interviews sought to evaluate whether teachers' attitudes towards teaching about loss, change and death had altered as a result of the project and how children had responded to the teaching.

Throughout the project teachers were willing to discuss their feelings although they were clearly very anxious anything which they said remained anonymous. The following extracts appear exactly as they were recorded and demonstrate a variety of personal and professional responses from the teachers involved. Any names used are pseudonyms.

The following five questions were asked:

- Do you feel the topics of loss, change and death have been appropriate subjects for the children you teach?
- What kinds of questions have the children asked about loss, change and death?
- How comfortable have you felt answering children's questions?
- Have any of the pupils in your class/school experienced loss, change or bereavement recently? How did you feel you coped?
- Will you continue to teach about loss, change and death within the RE curriculum?

Do you feel the topics of loss, change and death have been appropriate subjects for the children you teach?

Towards the end of the project there seemed to be a heightened awareness of how sensitively the subjects needed to be addressed, particularly where children in the same classroom represented cultural and religious differences: 'Some of the kids have got me tied up in knots about funerals. I'm frightened of getting it wrong and causing offence.'

Others were more confident:

We educate our children about birth, so why not educate them about death too? I believe children need to know about that if they are going to

Key Stage 1 Drawing on pupils' own experience of loss, change and death	Key Stage 2 Drawing on pupils' own experience of loss, change and death	Key Stage 3 Drawing on pupils' own experience of loss, change and death
Death in nature	Death in animals	Language of Death
– autumn	– accidental	– metaphor
– winter	– old age	– everyday conversations
– animals	– deliberate/food/research	– historical accounts
– plants	– characteristics of death	
Changes	Changes	Loss in human life
– new baby	– new school	– loss of health
– new siblings in family	– new teacher	– loss of friends
– starting school	– new friends	– primary/secondary school
– moving house	– family circumstances	transfer
	– growing older, ageing	– failing exams
		– redundancy
		– war/violence
Loss	Death in humans	Death in humans
– losing toys	– natural disasters	– stages of grief
– losing teeth	– old age and illness	– introduction to coping with
	– war and violence	death
		– fears and anxieties
Topics		
– what makes me feel happy/sad?		
– stages of life		
– my feelings		
Teaching about the beliefs of faith communities concerning what happens at the time of death and beyond	**Teaching about the beliefs of faith communities concerning what happens at the time of death and beyond**	**Teaching about the beliefs of faith communities concerning what happens at the time of death and beyond**
Probably not appropriate unless this is within the child's experience and in helping children to be aware that this is an area of faith which gives rise to very puzzling questions.	By the end of Key Stage 2 children should be aware that experiences in these areas can give rise to questions which have different answers and for some people these are to do with 'being with God'.	Beliefs of Christianity, Judaism, Sikhism, Islam, Buddhism and Hinduism and Humanism. N.B. use Agreed or Diocesan Syllabus as a guide.
N.B. Where this area is appropriate it is important that questions are answered as honestly and accurately as possible.	Beliefs of world religions. N.B. use Agreed or Diocesan Syllabus as a guide.	Suffering in world religions.

Figure 7.2 Exploring loss, change and death in the school curriculum

Cultural and organisational aspects of death and dying in the twentieth century	Cultural and organisational aspects of death and dying in the twentieth century	Cultural and organisational aspects of death and dying in the twentieth century
Probably not appropriate except in helping children to appreciate lives and deaths of religious and secular persons or where this is within a child's personal experience. N.B. Where this area is appropriate it is important that all questions are answered as honestly and accurately as possible.	Places where end of life happens: home, hospital, hospice Recording a death Undertakers	Places to rest before the funeral: – mortuary – chapel of rest – home – place of worship Graveyards and crematoria Arranging a funeral Community care agencies
Exploring loss, change and death in language, story and literature – own account of loss, change, death	**Exploring loss, change and death in language, story and literature** – stories of fantasy and fiction concerning life experiences; myths and legends; saints and martyrs.	**Exploring loss, change and death in language, story and literature** – funeral liturgies
– sharing picture/story books	– sacred writing – own poetry/prayers – death in the media e.g. TV; films	– sacred writings – humorous epitaphs – artwork; drama – novels; biographies
Exploring children's questions and concerns – what happens when something dies? – can things/animals/people come back to life? – will I die? will you die?	**Exploring children's questions and concerns** – what is a dead person like? – are people the same as plants and animals?	**Exploring children's questions and concerns** – What happens if a person dies? – How long can I expect to live? – Who would help me if someone in my family died? – What happens to a body after death?
	Moral Issues – use of animals for research – battery farming – animal slaughtering – treatment of elderly persons	Moral/Ethical Issues – organ donation – euthanasia – cryonics (freezing bodies) – medical definition of death – life support systems – death in war
	Ultimate Questions – why do people experience pain and suffering? – why do young people die? – is there life after death?	Ultimate Questions – why pain/suffering/terminal illness? – reconciling God and suffering – what happens when we die? – physical and religious answers – does the manner of death matter?

Figure 7.2 continued

	Related Themes – conflict	Related Themes – conflict – war and peace – salvation – liberation
Teaching about customs, rituals and practices associated with death and dying in world faiths Burying a pet Burial places	**Teaching about customs, rituals and practices associated with death and dying in world faiths** Burying a pet Memorials: religious and secular Symbols of death	**Teaching about customs, rituals and practices associated with death and dying in world faiths** Memorials; epitaphs; obituaries. Last rites and burial practices in world religions. N.B. use Agreed Syllabus as a guide.
Shared meals Celebrations Saying goodbye My life so far Marking special occasions	Death ceremonies in world religions. N.B. use Agreed Syllabus as a guide.	Disposal of the body in world religions.
	Related Themes – pilgrimage – memories – milestones in life	Related Themes – pilgrimage – death rites

Figure 7.2 continued

make sense of the world in which they are growing up. It isn't just about dying though – there is much more which we need to help children to discover for themselves. Things like being ill or when your parents are unemployed. Things like that really matter to children although people often think they are too young to understand.

What kinds of questions have the children asked about loss, change and death?

Throughout the implementation of the Schemes of Work children asked questions about death and dying. There were also many references to discussions outside Religious Education lessons. It would appear children in rural schools are more enquiring about the permanence and physical attributes of death and dying, whilst those children from homes where a variety of religious and cultural traditions are represented are more concerned with an afterlife. 'The kids came into school during a particularly cold spell and asked, "What happens to the lambs that die in the field after the birds and other animals have eaten their meat?"'

Teachers often commented on the challenge of children's questions such as 'How do you know when you are dead?' and the problems of attempting to answer questions of ultimate meaning such as 'Why is there pain and suffering?'

One teacher said:

The trouble is, children always catch you off your guard. Most of the things they have asked me have been at times other than when we were dealing with death. I think this is partly because the subject is no longer taboo they feel much easier about the whole thing. The most difficult thing a child has asked me was, 'How will there be enough room for all the people after they have died?'

Questions asked by other children included:

• How do you know when you are dead? (Year 2)
• How does anyone else know when you are dead? (Year 2)
• If I put that star fish in the water will it move again? (Year 1)
• Does dying hurt? (Year 5)

How comfortable have you felt answering children's questions?

Over three-quarters of the teachers interviewed said they still found pupils' questions difficult to answer. The replies contained phrases such as: 'struggled', 'felt baffled', 'answered the best way I could'. However, all agreed the in-service training had given them strategies for coping and two teachers said they would be 'as honest as possible' and 'not pretend you knew the answer if you didn't'.

A male teacher commented that he listened very carefully to what the child asked and then 'put the ball firmly in their court', asking 'What do you think happens?' Generally teachers seemed to have more confidence when they were asked factual questions. It was when they were faced with ones to which there are no definitive answers they felt challenged.

Have any of the pupils in your class/school experienced loss, change or bereavement recently? How did you feel you coped?

All of the teachers gave examples of children who had experienced loss, change or bereavement during the term in which the interviews took place. For instance: 'He is on his third Dad of the year.' 'A little girl in my class whose Mummy has just remarried has found she has cancer and the prognosis is not good.'

Teachers' personal experience of loss, change and death and their emotional response when children encounter grief appears to play a large part in how confident they feel about addressing the subject with children. One said: 'I wonder why it is children can make you feel so vulnerable yourself. Speaking to him about his grandfather's death brought back my own grief and how there is a big gap in my life.'

Ninety per cent of teachers said they felt more able to support children than they had at the beginning of the project. There were others who expressed frustration that they were unable to provide as much support as they would have liked:

> The younger child role-plays his absent father all the time he is in the home-corner. I'm at a complete loss as to what to do. He thinks his father is away working so until he is told the truth from his older brother or his friends, I'm stuck in a position where I am unable to facilitate any healing process.

> The National Curriculum seems to get in the way of the pastoral and Religious Education Curriculum.

Will you continue to teach about loss, change and death in the Religious Education curriculum?

All teachers who took part in the project were confident they would continue to develop what they were currently doing, although 75 per cent of these felt more in-service training opportunities were needed for other members of staff in their schools. 'We have found out for ourselves that unless people have support they shy away from the topic'.

Some people who would be teaching a different Key Stage the following academic year intended to encourage their colleagues to extend the experience which their children had already gained. A Year 6 teacher had liaised with the local secondary school and had persuaded the Religious Education Coordinator to continue the project when his pupils transferred school. Understandably there was also a note of caution expressed by just over ten per cent of teachers that: 'We don't spend a disproportionate amount of time on this and other areas of the pupils' Religious Education suffer as a result.'

At the start of the research teachers often talked about their fears of tackling a subject which they thought was 'taboo'. This endorses a long-held view that death is a topic to be avoided in polite conversation. However, at the end of the in-service training it became clear that when teachers were given an opportunity to explore their own attitudes, they felt better equipped to deal with the reactions and perceptions of children, which supports the findings of Solnit and Green (1988) and Tatelbaum (1980). Indeed, at the time the Schemes of Work were introduced into schools over eighty per cent said their awareness of children's emotional response to loss had been raised.

What the research tells us

The research findings generally support the view that young children are unable to grasp the permanence of death, believing a body in a dead state can change to a living state – 'My Dad has gone to heaven, but he will be back by the time we go on holiday'.

Teachers reported that most children at Key Stage 2 understood the permanence of death. This reflects the findings of Koochler (1973), Maurer (1961) and Anthony (1973), that a conceptual understanding of death is a developmental feature of children's intelligence. Furthermore the findings indicate that children living in rural locations enquired more deeply about the physical attributes of death. Conversely pupils attending schools where a range of faith and cultural traditions were represented were more concerned with what happened to a body after earthly life. The exception to this hypothesis was a group of children from ethnic minority groups who had a parent working at a teaching hospital. In this instance pupils' understanding of the physical attributes of death was greatly enhanced as well as their knowledge of the beliefs and practices of death and dying. There is a possible correlation here between either Judd's research (1989) which showed that when children are confronted with death they are likely to have a more mature understanding of mortality, or the work of Wenestam (1982) and Dyregrov (1991) who conclude that social and cultural environments influence children's thinking. Almost inevitably, where children have experience of death rituals and ceremonies their views about what happens after death are influenced by the religion to which they belong.

There were many instances throughout the project where children's emotional responses were evident. Over a quarter of the teachers used the words 'fear', 'anxious', 'scared', 'frightened', or 'apprehensive', to describe children's reactions where they encountered death at home or in the local community. Although it is recognised the words used to describe grief are adult adjectives, this seems to reflect the views of Worden (1988) and McNeill (1988) that many children perceive death as a disruptive and hostile event over which they have no control.

An important factor influencing children's ideas about death is the language of death and dying. There were several occasions described by teachers which imply young children who heard adults using words such as 'dead' or 'died' had a better understanding of the permanence of death. Where these words were heard and repeated by children in the early years they seemed to avoid speaking in euphemisms and metaphors when they transferred to secondary school. Past research has not addressed the question of how language may play an important part in children's conceptual and emotional development.

Although loss and death are universal features of human experience, adults, like children, have different feelings and fears. The findings of the research left little doubt that where loss and death are taboo subjects, adults are likely to feel less able to support children or to include the topic in the school curriculum. However, where teachers are helped to understand children's responses, and themes are included in the Religious Education curriculum, pupils seem to show interest and be motivated to ask questions relevant to their religious, cultural and family backgrounds.

It should be remembered that loss, change and death are only a fractional part of the content of syllabuses for Religious Education. Deciding on a school policy, planning a curriculum framework and implementing a Programme of Study does not happen overnight. Furthermore, existing frameworks in schools will need to be reviewed and updated in line with local and national guidelines. Time will tell whether the research continues to help teachers and pupils develop strategies which support them in the future. Whatever the future holds, the words which one little boy shared with me will not be forgotten:

> When I saw Jane crying I told her it was not good to keep her hurt inside. Me and her sat on the seat and she said she was scared of what would happen to her granny now she was in the coffin. I told her about my Dad's funeral. All the things about grown ups who cried too and the book my teacher and I made about the happy times we had before my Dad died. I'm going to help Jane write a book. Then we can share our minds with other children.

Framework for the development of a school policy

Deciding on the rationale

The agreed rationale will determine the approach adopted by the school. It is suggested schools make themselves familiar with the County or Diocesan Syllabus for Religious Education and any materials which support these documents.

Staff should decide on several clearly stated aims, appropriate to the age and ability of the pupils. It is important that all persons involved:

- are aware of the statutory nature of the Agreed Syllabus or Diocesan Syllabus for Religious Education;
- share the purpose of the policy;
- contribute towards the development of a shared educational philosophy;
- have a supportive forum in which to share their views and concerns;
- acknowledge the cultural and religious perspectives of the school and its community.

Deciding who coordinates the work

The RE Coordinator should liaise closely with the school management team. In addition the following persons should be consulted:

- teaching/non-teaching staff;
- Governors;
- parents;
- community or faith group representatives.

Carrying out initial research

It will be necessary to have information about children's present experience of loss and change and the kinds of future experiences which they are likely to encounter. Ideally the coordinator should have attended training concerning loss, change and grief in children's lives. Where this is not the case, information may be obtained through:

- discussion with colleagues, parents and professionals;
- questionnaires;
- reference material.

Drafting the policy

If the consultation process is to be considered valuable, those involved need to feel their views are heard and appropriate revision should be made to the draft policy. It is important to keep an educational perspective whilst also considering the rights and views of other persons such as parents and community members. Outside advice may need to be sought and it is inevitable that there will be compromise.

Dissemination and implementation of the policy

Once the document is agreed, it should be circulated as widely as possible to ensure that all concerned recognise it as the *school policy*. To this end, the curriculum and practice must consistently and clearly reflect the document. However it is important that the dissemination process is an ongoing one which allows for new initiatives and developments.

Document review and continuing development

The following should be taken into account:

- Naming the person responsible for the review.
- The format of the review e.g. meetings.
- The in-service training of staff.
- New government, county, diocesan or community developments as they arise.

There follows an example of an LEA policy statement.

OXFORDSHIRE COUNTY SCHOOL POLICY STATEMENT FOR INCLUDING ASPECTS OF LOSS, CHANGE AND DEATH IN THE RELIGIOUS EDUCATION CURRICULUM

1. This policy statement was agreed on 6/1/1998 by the staff and governing body of .... , after the following meetings of the governing body/working party:

14/6/1997
30/6/1997
13/9/1997
22/11/1997

2. The staff and governing body of .... School believe that helping children to learn about and to understand loss and change is an essential and integral part of a 'balanced and broadly-based' school curriculum. This includes the subject of death and dying which is part of the Agreed Syllabus for Religious Education. The curriculum aims to help pupils:

- to be aware of, and to respond to, life experiences and the questions they raise.
- to know about and to understand religious beliefs and practices from birth to death.
- to develop positive attitudes towards other people.

3. The content of the school policy takes into account the views of:

- Teaching staff.
- Parents.
- School governors.
- Community members (local and wider).
- Religious organisations and community agencies.
- LEA representatives.

4. In-service training has been undertaken by staff planning and implementing the scheme of work.

5. The school has a scheme of work which reflects this policy statement. The curriculum content is appropriate to children at Key Stages 1–3. The framework includes Key Stage 3 because we see it as our role to support pupils as they transfer to secondary education. The host secondary schools have received a copy of the scheme of work and policy statement.

6. The school programme includes the following elements:

- Exploring loss, change and death within the pupils' experience, and answering questions and concerns.
- Learning about the main beliefs of world religions and the expression of these beliefs through ceremonies and customs.
- Cultural and organisational factors especially when these are motivated by social, religious and ethical values.
- The expression of religious belief through literature, language and the creative and expressive arts.

7. The content and organisation of the school curriculum will be reviewed annually. It will take into account new government, county, diocesan and community initiatives and legislation.

Chapter 8

Managing a Critical Incident in School

In recent years there have been several disasters and tragedies which have affected schools and pupils. There is also a growing awareness of loss and change in children's lives. Events like these have an impact on adults and pupils although the emotional effects are not always immediately apparent.

At a time when schools are increasingly under pressure to ensure the academic performance of their pupils, the pastoral care of children may not appear to be a priority. An attitude seems to prevail which assumes tragedies and disasters happen to other people. There is of course a sense of security in this thought, but if schools are to fulfil their pastoral responsibilities and increase their effectiveness, they also need to be pro-active in the development of strategic plans for crisis situations. This will enable them to respond to traumatic events and disasters quickly and effectively.

There are several reasons why schools should be the catalyst for this approach and not rely solely on support services and outside agencies. School staff:

- know the members of the school community;
- have expertise in meeting the individual needs of pupils;
- are familiar with school organisation and routines;
- are more likely to respect the privacy of adults and children.

Although the effects of traumatic events are unique to the communities in which they occur, there are some general principles described by authors such as Yule and Gold (1993) and Dyregrov (1991) which schools will find helpful. (see Figure 8.1).

Within the context of the framework which is offered, in this book, 'traumatic experience' takes into account the effects on pupils, their families and staff of:

- the sudden death of someone known to them;
- the involvement of pupils or staff in an accident whilst out of school e.g. traffic accident, fire, drowning;
- an incident in school such as a shooting, fire or physical attack;
- the effects of social violence.

MANAGING A CRITICAL INCIDENT IN SCHOOL	
	Time-scale
FIRST PRIORITY	
• Obtain factual information at start of crisis	within hours
• Senior management meet with school staff	within hours
• Intervention team established	within hours
• Contact families (as appropriate)	within hours
SECONDARY PRIORITY	
• Call a staff meeting to give information	same day if practicable
• Inform pupils in small groups (as appropriate)	same day if practicable
• Call a debriefing meeting of staff involved in the crisis/disaster (as appropriate)	same day if practicable
• Debrief pupils involved in crisis/disaster (as appropriate)	as soon as possible
• Identify high risk pupils and staff	as soon as possible
ONGOING TASKS	
• Promote discussion in pupil groups	next few days and weeks
• Identify need for individual/group counselling or other help	next few days/weeks
• Organise any counselling/ support	as required
	Based on Yule and Gold (1993)

Figure 8.1 General principles for action

The strategic plan – first steps

Many schools who have had first-hand experience of traumatic events have reflected on their response to what happened and developed a strategic plan for the future. As with the framework for including teaching about loss, change and grief in the school curriculum, the initial planning process can be a lengthy one. It is however important that all staff are involved so that they are familiar with the framework and they own it as the school policy.

Deciding on the rationale

The rationale will determine the way in which individual schools respond. The objectives should take into account the ethos of the school as it is written in the school prospectus. It is important all persons involved:

- share the purpose of the strategic plan;
- contribute towards the development of the strategic plan;
- have a supportive forum in which to share their views and concerns;
- are familiar with human response to loss, change and grief in both adults and children;
- are aware of the religious and cultural backgrounds of the families represented in the school.

Deciding who coordinates the work

It is suggested that a member of the school management team coordinates the development of the strategic plan. The following people should be actively involved:

- the head teacher and all members of teaching and non-teaching staff;
- the school Governors;
- parent representatives;
- community and faith group representatives.

Initial planning, drafting and dissemination of the plan

There are a number of publications which suggest strategies for coping with crises in schools. Perhaps the best known of these is the book mailed to every school in the United Kingdom during 1993, *'Wise Before the Event' – Coping with Crises in Schools*, written by Yule and Gold and published by The Calouste Gulbenkian Foundation. The person with responsibility for coordinating the strategic plan should make himself familiar with this publication and particularly the types of events which might occur in a school. Any events which are not listed but have already been experienced by the school should also be noted.

Ideally, the coordinator should have attended in-service training concerning loss, change and grief in children's lives. Where this is not the case, training may be obtained from organisations and agencies listed at the end of this book.

A period of consultation will be necessary so that everyone involved feels their views have been taken into account. It is important to keep an educational perspective whilst also considering the rights and views of other persons such as parents and community members.

Once the document is agreed, it should be circulated to *all staff in the school*. It is recommended it is easily accessible so that it can be referred to if an incident occurs.

Responsibilities apportioned and training given as appropriate

Yule and Gold (1993) suggest that members of staff should be allocated responsibilities. The chart 'Managing a Critical Incident in School' (see Figure 8.1) is based on the model used by the above authors but has been divided according to management priorities. It is discussed in detail later in this chapter.

Review and continuing development

The following should be taken into account:

- Naming the person responsible for the review
- The timescale between reviews
- The format of the review
- How the content and purpose will be shared with new staff
- Any Government or local guidance.

First priorities in following the framework

- Obtain factual information.
- Senior management meet with school staff.
- Intervention team established.
- Contact families (as appropriate).

Obtaining factual information

After a major incident it may be very difficult to establish accurate details of what has happened, particularly if the event occurred outside the school community. Establishing facts is very important because rumours can exacerbate distress. Communication between the school and any staff who are with children off site is a priority. Therefore schools should consider having more than one telephone line so that one may be designated as an emergency communication link if the need arises. Where this is not possible, a mobile telephone may be useful. Remember that reception may be poor.

Senior management meet with school staff

As soon as an incident has been confirmed, senior management should meet to establish as much factual information as possible so this can be shared with the remainder of the school staff. It is preferable to bring all personnel together, but whether this is possible or not will depend on the size of the school and the availability of staff.

Senior management should take responsibility for:

- dealing with telephone enquiries from parents or relatives, giving them emergency contact numbers where necessary e.g hospital, emergency disaster number;
- contacting the parents of children involved in the incident and advise them how further information will be conveyed;
- dealing with enquiries from the media.

Intervention team established

Senior management should establish an intervention team to activate agreed strategies. This will include:

- meeting parents who come to the school seeking more information and staying with them;
- arranging transport for parents who need to get to school;
- persons who will maintain normal routines as far as possible and make sure the welfare of pupils in the school is given priority;
- persons to liaise with others who have heard about the incident and come to the school.

Contact families and reunite children with parents

Children who have witnessed the event or been involved in the incident should be reunited with their families as soon as possible after any emergency intervention has taken place by medical or rescue services. Whether parents are able to be taken to the scene of the event will depend on how accessible it is to the school. If it is impossible to reunite families, senior management should do everything possible to establish telephone contact between young people and their parents.

Second priorities

- Calling a staff meeting and giving information.
- Dealing with the media.
- Informing pupils in small groups (as appropriate).
- Calling a debriefing meeting of staff involved in the crisis/disaster (as appropriate).
- Debriefing pupils involved in the crisis/disaster (as appropriate).
- Identifying high risk pupils and staff.
- Adjusting to normal routines.

Calling a staff meeting and giving information

Where it has been possible to share information with all school staff soon after the event, it is important that the initial information is updated and clarified at regular intervals. Where some staff do not know what has happened, senior management should call a meeting of all those who still need to be informed. No one on the staff should be excluded from this meeting since there will be tremendous pressure from parents, the local community and the media for information. Neither should the ongoing care and support of members of staff who have been the most affected by the incident fall to one or two senior managers in the school. In some cases it may be helpful to seek support from outside agencies, but generally, long-term support is best shared by members of the school community. Where outside support is sought, it should build on the efforts of the school staff and not seek to replace them. Where school staff have had professional development concerning the effects of loss, change and grief, the school community is more likely to be able to recognise its needs and to support individual persons.

Dealing with the media

When a traumatic event happens, it is likely the school will become the focus of attention. Schools have a pastoral responsibility to shield pupils and families from as much intrusion as possible. Therefore it is wise to appoint a senior member of staff who will take responsibility for the management of the media. Alternatively, the local education authority may provide personnel who will fulfil this role. Generally it is unwise to allow members of the press into the school.

Informing pupils in small groups (as appropriate)

Children need clear, accurate information if they are to begin to make sense of what has happened. Where possible, class teachers or form tutors are probably the best people to break the news, since they know the pupils and will have established good communication with them in the past. Pupils should only be told information which is factual in order to prevent confusion and rumours. Figure 8.2 sets out the points to be considered. Written information should also be sent home to parents via their child.

Calling a debriefing meeting of staff involved in the crisis/disaster

Many schools who have been involved in a traumatic event speak of the importance of bringing all those persons directly involved together as soon as possible after the incident. A debriefing meeting may help to:

- clarify what happened;
- reassure people that their feelings and responses are normal;
- identify people in need of specialist support from outside agencies.

Debriefing pupils involved in the crisis (as appropriate)

Adults will need to make themselves available to pupils who wish to talk about the event and children should be encouraged to do this although nobody should be forced to do so. After a few days have elapsed many pupils will welcome a return to normal school routines but they should feel secure in the knowledge that staff are still available to listen to their concerns in the days and weeks ahead.

Breaking sad news to an individual child	Breaking sad news to groups of children
Who should tell the child? • Someone who is known and trusted by the child. • Someone who can maintain contact with the child in the time ahead. • Someone who has a sound knowledge of how children respond to loss, change and grief. • Someone who allows the child to express their feelings. **Where should the child be told?** • In a familiar place. • In safe and comfortable surroundings. • In a private place. **How should the news be given?** • In language which is easily understood. • In language which is factual. • With opportunities for the child to ask questions. • With opportunities for the child to show emotional responses. • With an opportunity for the adult to establish the child has understood the news which has been given.	**Who should tell the children?** • Someone who is known and trusted by the children. • Someone who is confident speaking to the group. • Someone who has sound knowledge of how children respond to loss, change and grief. • Someone who respects children's confidentiality. **How should children be told?** • In a familiar setting, preferably a classroom, rather than a large hall. • In language which is easily understood by them. • By giving them factual information which is consistent with information which other children in the school are given. • With sufficient time available to answer questions and raise concerns.

Figure 8.2 Breaking sad news

Identifying high risk pupils and staff

Schools will find it useful to designate a member of staff to fulfil the role of a supportive-carer for pupils and adults. It is important to recognise that each person involved in the traumatic event will have an individual response. Where schools have taken part in professional development which has made reference to post-traumatic stress disorders, they will be better equipped to recognise adults and children who may be at high risk. If children or adults have died, it is essential the school acknowledges this and extends sympathy to the families concerned. In most cases bereaved families will appreciate representatives from the school at funerals.

Adjusting to normal routines

In the immediate aftermath of a traumatic event it is essential to acknowledge what has happened and to give people opportunities to express their feelings and to reflect on the fact that life will never be the same again. But it is also important to establish normal routines so that pupils feel secure. Where children return to school soon afterwards, they may still be suffering from shock and trauma. The following may help:

- Listening to worries and concerns.
- Allowing part-time attendance at first.
- Making arrangements for a quiet place either with or without an adult if this is desired.
- Reassurance that extra support will be given if a child's academic performance has suffered.
- Reassurance that help from outside the school can be sought if the child and their parents desire this.
- Encouraging children to be patient in their reactions.

Ongoing tasks

- Promote discussion in pupil groups.
- Identify need for individual/group counselling or other help.

Promoting discussion in pupil groups

Although individual schools should adopt a policy which will support children from the time of the traumatic event and meet their individual needs, the following framework for promoting discussion in pupil groups may be helpful. The facilitator should have a sound knowledge of children's responses to loss, change and grief.

Stage 1 – Explaining the purpose of the meeting

The setting where children are introduced to discussion groups should be familiar to them and should be facilitated by their own teacher or form tutor wherever possible. Confidentiality should be established at the onset of the discussion and pupils should be reassured they may express their feelings in any way they wish as long as they are not hurting themselves or anyone else. Although all who are present are invited to participate in the meeting there is no expectation that everyone will speak or contribute if they do not wish to do so.

Stage 2 – Children telling what they know about the event

At this stage pupils are encouraged to share with the adult what they know about the trauma. Therefore it is important this person has a thorough and accurate knowledge of what happened so that any misunderstandings or confusion can be clarified. Providing children with concrete information helps them to come to terms with what has happened and to allay any misconceptions or rumours.

Stage 3 – Describing feelings at the time of the event

Helping children to articulate the way they felt when they first heard about the event or witnessed what was happening provides a bridge between the event and the emotional responses which have developed afterwards. It is important that where children are asked any questions these are open-ended, encouraging them to reveal as much or as little as they wish.

Stage 4 – Sharing feelings experienced between the event and the present time

When children are encouraged to share their feelings soon after the event, they are more likely to be able to identify their responses up to the present time. Because emotions may be difficult to describe and the intensity of the feelings may be very powerful, hearing how other people have responded may help individual children to feel less isolated and more in control. Putting thoughts into words can be very helpful, but some pupils may prefer to draw or to write about the event. Young children may 'play out' what happened.

Stage 5 – Collecting thoughts together and describing individual and group responses

At this stage, the role of the adult is to summarise what actually happened and to describe the thoughts and feelings which have been shared by the children. Reassurance should be given to individuals and to the group that their responses will vary and the intensity of emotions may be greater at some times than at others.

Stage 6 – Looking to the future

Because children may feel very vulnerable after a tragic event, it is important they are helped to feel safe and to be given opportunities to plan what will happen in the time ahead. In the short term this may include attending funerals, deciding on memorials or some other way of marking what has happened.

Identifying the need for individual or group counselling or other help

Children and staff who have been involved in a traumatic event will take time adjusting to what has happened. Generally those people whose lives were at greatest risk are likely to suffer the most stress and trauma. In addition, where victims have home circumstances which are unsettled, or in the case of persons with special educational needs, the likelihood of post-traumatic stress disorders seems to be increased. Thoughts and memories of the event will often monopolise their thoughts. In children the effects of grief can lead to a lack of concentration, changed behaviour and a decline in their academic performance. Physical illnesses such as headaches, stomach upsets and joint pains may also occur. Where children are lacking information about how an event occurred, fantasies may result which can be extremely distressing.

Problems are particularly likely and prolonged where siblings or peers have been injured or killed and children have been unable to receive the support they have needed after the event (Van Eerdewegh *et al.*, 1985). In extreme cases children may lose confidence in their own future, because they feel vulnerable and fearful that the event may recur (Dyregrov 1991). This is more likely where children witness social violence and warfare.

The developmental level of children seems to have a bearing on how their behaviour may be changed. Younger children may be less independent than they were before the event and they are more likely to regress in skills which have already been mastered. Likewise, older children often demonstrate behaviour which was characteristic of themselves at a younger age.

Some children will find great difficulty relating to their peer group and they may feel different and be prone to bullying or teasing. In addition, because friends may not know how to respond, they may avoid the child who is grieving which results in social isolation (Abrams 1992).

The way in which children experience a trauma or are told about it plays a large part in their reactions. Whatever the circumstances, they will need time to adjust and to work through both the event and their grief responses to the event. Dyregrov (1991) believes the problems which many children encounter in their grief are related to the circumstances of the event.

Responses to trauma may be shown through:
- Physical, emotional or developmental delay
- Fear of new situations

- Changed behaviour, for example hair twisting, thumb sucking, rocking
- Self-injury
- Extremes of passivity or aggression
- Stealing
- Fantasies
- Incontinence
- Eating disorders
- Personality changes
- Pessimism about the future
- Poor self-esteem

Many of the principles already discussed which relate to caring for bereaved children will be relevant to children recovering from a traumatic event. Some of the advantages of facilitating discussion between pupils in small groups has been outlined earlier in the chapter. Sometimes pupils will need additional support from outside the school which will encourage them to develop coping strategies. Schools do, however, have a responsibility towards families as well as towards the pupils in their care. It is essential the parents of pupils are consulted together with the young people themselves before help is sought from outside agencies. Furthermore, the reliability of support services and the experience and qualifications of individuals should be checked before they are invited to the school.

Essentially the role of support services should be to build on the caring role of the school and the skills possessed by the staff, rather than attempting to replace these. Yule and Gold (1993) describe what they call 'ground rules to observe when working with outside consultants'. These include:

- Agreeing the boundaries of confidential information.
- Clarifying personnel to be informed when concern is raised about a child.
- Facilitating regular meetings between any support agencies and teaching staff.

Perhaps the most important strategy to adopt is to listen to what individual people say about what they want, rather than assuming a need. Empathy and compassion are human capacities but they are developed through practice more often than they are learned through the pages of textbooks. The schools, families and individuals with whom I have been privileged to work have reminded me over and over again that people who are in distress need information which is communicated to them clearly, an element of control over what is going on in their lives and permission to grieve in the way which is best for them. This involves helping people to understand the role which a person may have and outlining the support which they are able to give and whether the support will be ongoing.

Many support agencies will have people working for them who have expertise in helping people to adapt to loss, change and grief, but almost without exception people who are already known to individuals will provide better support than personnel who may imagine themselves to be the 'experts'.

Responding to sad events in school

From the early days of childhood most children form friendships and as they grow older relationships develop which may be extremely intense and long-lasting. When a peer dies children's grief is not unlike that associated with the death of a sibling. The death is seen to be unjust and untimely; hence it may trigger bitter feelings, coupled with a sense of loneliness and isolation. It is quite normal for children to reflect on how the situation might have been if it was themselves who had died. This happens especially if the death occurred in violent or tragic circumstances or if the place of death was one which friends had frequented.

Where a child is life-threatened or terminally ill, preparing the remainder of the pupils for what will happen is very important, especially if the illness or medication results in a changed physical appearance. Young children will also need reassurance that not all sickness results in death.

Each child is part of a school family in addition to belonging to their home. Therefore it is important that if a child or someone known to the school community dies, people are able to express their sadness and to acknowledge how the contribution which the person made to the community will be remembered.

Parents need to know how a school has responded and what information has been given to their child. This will include:

- Factual information about the circumstances of the illness or death
- Information about how their child may respond after hearing the news
- Suggestions for books which may help their child understand the event.

Rituals and ceremonies

Children need to participate in rituals and ceremonies since these events will give concrete expression to their thoughts and feelings. It also allows them to acknowledge what has happened and to confront the reality of their loss. But for ceremonies to be a helpful part of coming to terms with what has happened, children should be involved as much or as little as they wish. Adults need to have their views respected too, especially since there are a great variety of cultural and religious views concerning children and funeral rites. Parents should never be persuaded against their wishes to let a child go to a funeral. Neither should a child be forced to go. However, children who have had an opportunity to attend are generally glad they went. Those who were prevented may grow up to regret they were not given the choice.

How should schools respond to bereaved families?
- Maintain contact and express sympathy.
- Be aware of cultural and religious beliefs or practices.
- Encourage the family to maintain control over any decisions which need to be made.
- Respect privacy where this is requested.

If families conduct private funerals, schools may choose to hold a memorial service, where children are encouraged to take an active part in how they will say 'goodbye'. If the death occurred in traumatic circumstances, a ceremony may prove to be therapeutic, signifying that the event is over. Although people feel sad, the school community is able to plan for the future.

How might schools respond?
- Suggesting pupils and staff representatives who might attend the funeral.
- Arranging a special assembly or an act of collective worship in school.
- Arranging a memorial service in school and encouraging pupils to contribute.
- Lighting a candle which burns between the death and the funeral; providing a tangible memorial such as planting a tree or making a memory book; marking the anniversary of the death.

Chapter 9

Ceremonies, Rites and Rituals of Death and Mourning

Introduction

In the body, a million births and deaths take place at every moment. The body is a miracle of re-birth in which our habits, our likes and dislikes, our hunger, and our states of mind are always driving the body towards change and development. Never for an instant does the body cease to die, cease to be born. We might say that we live through death at every moment.

Prickett (1980)

Birth and death are the two events which come to every human being and all religions are concerned with them. Belief in survival beyond death is perhaps the oldest religious conviction of humankind. Far back in prehistoric times traces remain of such an idea, in the way in which bodies were buried and in which tools and ornaments were laid beside them for use in the life to come. There is a great variety of teaching in world religions about death and its consequences; from the resurrection taught by monotheistic faiths to the reincarnation held by the religions of India and beyond, but all believe that there is more to human existence than the statutory three score years and ten. In sacred scriptures two kinds of death are spoken about: physical death and spiritual death. The former is of great importance to all people but the latter is of much greater significance. The first part of this chapter attempts to outline the development of belief about dying and to offer some information concerning death and funeral rites in Great Britain in the twentieth century. The second part describes beliefs and practices concerning death and dying in world religions.

Rites and rituals: an historical outline

As long as sixty thousand years ago, there was a belief in life after death and a deeply rooted sense of an underlying spiritual dimension of life. Mourning became part of the expression of grief at the close of earthly life. It was reflected in concern and sadness for the deceased. The way in which ceremonies, rites and rituals once affected every aspect of life is hard for us to imagine today. In the ancient Chinese religions people buried their dead in chambers furnished with paintings, carvings and lacquered timber, together with swords, jewellery, combs, chopsticks and mirrors. Today we do not believe that the dead will be able to use objects which we bury with them. However, the gifts of wreaths and flowers remain an important part of funeral rites.

In Victorian times when a member of the royal family died, those with any social pretensions went into public mourning, and private mourning extended beyond the immediate family members to the servants' hall and to tenants' cottages. Queen Victoria is said to have been 'quite shocked' that her five month old granddaughter in the Prussian court was not in mourning in 1859 after the death of her great-grandmother. She suggested that the baby should be dressed in white or lilac and that her nurses should wear grey or 'drab'. Even as we approach the twenty-first century the private sentiments of the royal family are often outweighed by consideration of what civil society expects. There needs to be an opportunity to give the public the chance to pay homage. The death of the late Princess of Wales bears witness to this.

In Great Britain we still have evidence of the common practice of wealthy persons to erect large tombs and family vaults. The enormous importance attached to this is perhaps best understood in the light of the literal Christian belief in the resurrection of the body. As late as 1829 publicity was given to a serious proposal to erect a London pyramid, four times higher than St. Paul's Cathedral, with the capacity for 10 million coffins.

The importance of mourning dress extended into the twentieth century, but black was by no means the only colour involved. Relatives at the funerals of spinsters and bachelors or children often wore white, white gloves, scarves and hat bands. White feathers and velvet adorned the hearse and coffin too. In general, deep mourning dress was observed by widows for a year and a day after death (presumably the extra day was required because the anniversary of the death could not have been an appropriate day on which to make any change). During this time a veil was worn outside the home and a widow's cap and weeper cuffs indoors.

The second year of mourning required drab colours with a minimum of jewellery and a gradual return to brighter hues. Mourning jewellery often preserved a relic of the deceased, such as a lock of hair, and in Victorian England marble replicas of hands and arms of deceased children were cherished by bereaved parents. Mourning extended not only to articles of dress and jewellery however, but to accessories such as parasols and handkerchiefs. There were items such as mourning writing paper, tea services, night caps, sweet bags and combs. Old-fashioned funerals which gave an opportunity for a wide variety of 'acting out' were undoubtedly far more therapeutic than those which modern life substitutes. It is clear that our ancestors acquired deep insight into the emotions and needs of people.

The first recorded person in England to trade as an undertaker was William Boyce who opened a shop in 1675 in London with a sign showing a suspended coffin and a figure of 'Time'. There were no written rules or code of practice in the early years of the trade. Anyone could set themselves up as a coffin maker or undertaker. However the funeral trade gradually increased and by the mid 1730s, funeral invitations were issued, often depicting a shrouded skeleton, representing 'Death'. Most coffin makers, undertakers and funeral furnishers had their premises away from busy thoroughfares and did not advertise their trade in the front of their building. Mr Sowerberry in Charles Dickens' *Oliver Twist* (1846) bears witness to the fact that many undertakers traded in insalubrious buildings:

> Oliver, being left to himself in the undertaker's shop, set the lamp down on a workman's bench, and gazed timidly about him with a feeling of awe and dread, which many people a good deal older than he will be at no loss to understand. An unfinished coffin on black trestles, which stood in the middle of the shop, looked so gloomy and death-like that a cold tremble came over him, everytime his eyes wandered in the direction of the dismal object: from which he almost expected to see a frightful form slowly rear its head, to drive him mad with terror. Against the wall were ranged, in regular array, a long row of elm boards cut into the same shape: looking, in the dim light, like high shouldered ghosts with their hands in their breeches' pocket. Coffin plates, elm chips, bright headed nails, and shreds of black cloth, lay scattered on the floor; and a wall behind the counter was ornamented with a lively representation of two mutes in very stiff-necked cloths, on duty at a large private door, with a hearse drawn by four black steeds, approaching in the distance. The shop was close and hot. The atmosphere seemed tainted with the smell of coffins. The recess beneath the counter in which his flock mattress was thrust looked like a grave.

There were, however, exceptions to the rule. A coffin maker and furnisher undertaker in 1838 had a nine page catalogue listing thirty designs of coffin, twenty sizes of shroud (available in different qualities of material), coffin mattresses, and palls. Seventeen shillings would buy 'a good elm coffin, furnished with a row of black or white nails, an inscription plate, four handles, silk lining and a pillow, whilst for nine pounds one could buy the pièce de résistance – a one and a half inch oak case, covered with cloth, furnished with three rows of best nails, six ornamental diamonds, a brass plate, and four pairs of best cherub handles.' The cost of a town funeral was two pounds and three shillings including a carriage drawn by two horses.

By the middle of the nineteenth century funerals were often very elaborate. Funeral furnishers had amalgamated with the original coffin makers and undertakers into a single trade of 'funeral director' or 'undertaker' founded in 1905.

Much of life is made up of rituals but these are so much part of everyday activity that we do not necessarily think about their origins or their meanings. If we pass a church and see a row of black cars and a special car filled with flowers we know that someone has died, because a message is acted out in such a way that there is instant recognition of the process. Indeed part of the importance of the 'acting out' is that there is little need to explain. Ceremonial processes are rich in symbolism. In the symbolic forms of expression, a variety of non-verbal ways of expressing feelings come into play. All cultures from the most primitive to the most sophisticated seem to use these forms of ritualised expression to surround important events. In other words, we need ceremonial activity to give us a chance to act out the feelings that are too deep to be expressed verbally.

The coming together at a funeral of family, friends and community, is a statement of sustaining love and respect that is ongoing even though a person has died. Those who watch what takes place are constantly made aware of the fact that what is important is not so much what is said at such times as what is implied by the coming together. The more ceremony and ritual that is present, the more opportunities there are for the expression of feelings.

Christianity

Christians believe mortal life ends in death and that the earthly body is cast aside so that a person may become immortal. There are, however, different beliefs and emphases within Christianity regarding what actually happens at death, and what happens afterwards. To understand this fully it is necessary to grasp the historical roots of the Christian tradition.

In Biblical times there was a clear connection between sin and death because sin had no place in the presence of the perfection of God. Death was not regarded as the end, however. Rather, it was seen as the joining of the souls in the underworld (sheol). When a person died they were gathered to their forefathers and dwelt with them in sheol which was a place cut off from the presence of God and from the land of the living. (Psalm 88: v. 5–6, v. 10–12). In Jesus' time virtually all Jewish groups except the Sadducees acknowledged some notion of resurrection beyond death and believed that at some stage there would be a division between the righteous and the unrighteous who would lead separate existences.

In the Synoptic Gospels (Matthew, Mark, Luke), three points stand out clearly in Jesus' teaching about death.

1. Willingness to endure death for Jesus' sake is the supreme test of faith (Luke 14: 26).
2. Death is the end of all earthly pleasures, activities and sufferings.
3. Death marks the beginning of eternal life.

From the beginning, Christianity was distinctive in its belief in the resurrection of Jesus, and early Christians preached about Jesus and the resurrection. All four evangelists affirm that Jesus died and rose, and in the New Testament and Christian history most accounts of his death at the

Crucifixion include his giving up of the spirit and the piercing of his side with a spear so that blood and water came out. (Matthew 27: 32–56, Mark 15: 21–41, Luke 23: 2–49, John 19: 17–37). The Apostles' Creed affirms this belief in the words, 'crucified, dead, buried, descended into hell'.

The resurrection of Jesus was always affirmed by contemporary Christians, and Paul in his letter to the church in Corinth (1 Cor: 15) lists all those who were witnesses to the appearances of Jesus saying 'if the dead are not raised, neither has Christ been raised; and if Christ has not been raised, your faith is in vain and you are still in your sins'.

Early Christians spoke of death as 'sleep'. When Stephen had been stoned, he prayed to the Lord to receive his spirit and not blame his persecutors. The theology of death was worked out by Paul (1 Cor: 15), parts of which are still used in the funeral service today. For Paul a number of things were quite clear.

- Death was the final enemy which had to be conquered because death was the logical consequence of sin.
- Death had been conquered by the resurrection of Jesus.
- As God incorporated himself into man's death by becoming incarnate, so humankind was incorporated or baptised into his infinite and eternal life in Jesus' resurrection.
- The resurrection of the body refers to the spiritual body; it does not require the earthly body for its housing.
- Christians will share Christ's risen life in the fullness of time.

In the early church, burials were joyful occasions with the relatives dressed in white, celebrating the certainty of the resurrection. However, as the centuries passed, the attitudes towards death and the hope in an afterlife underwent changes. Burials became occasions for mourning and the clothes of the relatives changed from white to black. There was an emphasis on a final judgement, reflected for example in mystery plays.

Pictures of heaven and hell in Christian mythology were partly influenced by Jewish ideas and the book of Revelation describes 'the throne of God in heaven' with a sea of glass in front of it and round it four creatures with eyes and wings. Hell is described as a bottomless pit where Satan is bound with his angels.

Today this imagery is not taken literally by all people, and it was tempered in the early Orthodox and the Western Catholic church by the notion of purgatory or an intermediate place. Protestants reject this doctrine of purgatory although prayers for the memory of the dead are still offered by some Anglicans. Christianity inherited the practice of burying the dead from Judaism. The most famous early Christian burial places are the catacombs in Rome.

By the middle ages, an elaborate pattern of services for the dead had developed in Western Christendom. During the preparation of the body for burial, psalms and prayers were said commending the souls of the dead to the mercy of God and these prayers were repeated whilst the body was carried to the church for the funeral service. The coffin was sprinkled with holy water before a procession to the grave and the burial. A bell often tolled at the funeral as a reminder of human mortality. Memorial services and masses continued to be said in church, particularly on the 3rd, 9th and 13th day after the death.

Protestant funeral rites

These services are usually brief but they lay great stress on the hope of the resurrection. The opening sentences of the funeral service in most Christian traditions speak of this hope: 'I am the resurrection and the life, said the Lord: he that believeth in me, though he were dead, yet shall he live and whosoever liveth and believeth in me shall never die' (John 11: 25 onwards).

In the majority of traditions the service does not include prayers for the soul of the departed. The destiny of the soul is left in God's hands. Prayers include thanks for the life that has been lived and for new life which has been promised. Sermons usually refer to the resurrection and the promise of eternal life and St. Paul's discourse on the resurrection of the body will also be read. Whether the body is buried or cremated will largely depend on the attitude of the deceased's family towards death, and it is impossible to generalise about this.

The Roman Catholic tradition

Roman Catholics pray for those who die with their lives spiritually unfinished and accept the doctrine of purgation of death, when the soul is purified by some form of suffering. Purgatory is not, however, a form of punishment. It is a process through which the human will is purified through prayer to make heaven possible. Catholics ask for the intercession of Mary and all the saints in this process of purgation.

The funeral mass is usually celebrated in purple vestments and the theme is the resurrection of Christ, with the emphasis not on fear or loss, but on Christian hope. This service precedes the final commendation and farewell, which begins with the words, 'It is our solemn duty to carry out, in the traditional manner of God's faithful people, the burial of this mortal body. As we do so, we can trust fully upon God from whom all creation has life. May He in due time in His power, bring to resurrection with all the saints, the body of this our brother or sister.' The coffin is then sprinkled with holy water and prayers or psalms are said before the procession to the place of burial. The grave may be blessed. As the coffin is lowered into the ground, the priest may say, 'It has pleased almighty God to call our brother/sister from this life to Himself. Accordingly we commit his/her body to the earth whence it came.'

Anglican funeral rites

Anglican rites include much from the Protestant tradition but the emphasis is on the hope of the resurrection. Generally there is a set liturgical service of psalms, bible readings and prayers. The deceased is entrusted to God's keeping and some high Anglican churches will include aspects of the Roman Catholic tradition, such as prayers for the soul of the dead person. A Requiem Mass may also be said or sung.

A memorial service of thanksgiving after a private burial or cremation is quite common. Whether the body is buried or cremated largely depends on any preference which the person may have expressed before death or on the attitude of the relatives.

In summary, most churches of the Anglican tradition concentrate on the following:

- There is uncertainty about what really happens after death.
- The human soul lives on, as in Paul's writing of the resurrection.
- The faithful departed are entrusted into the hands of God.
- The needs of the bereaved are the most urgent since something can be done about them.

Eastern Orthodox tradition

When an Eastern Orthodox Christian dies the body is washed after the custom described in the Bible (Acts 9: 37). It is then clothed in new garments. Psalms may be said over the body of an Orthodox believer from their death to the time of burial. At funerals, four standard candle sticks are placed at the four sides of the coffin, forming a cross. The mourners hold tapers which signify the light of Christian baptism and the light of the world to come. After a lengthy service of joy and thanksgiving the mortal remains are buried.

Sikhism

Many of the 35,000 Sikhs living in the United Kingdom are of Punjabi ethnic origin and Punjabi is often spoken in Sikh communities. In Sikhism references to death are often found associated with birth and the words janum (birth) and moran (death) generally occur together. According to Sikh belief humankind is not born sinful but in the grace of God which gives the soul the opportunity to become 'God in Flesh'. Neither is the person born free however. They are born to be free through breaking the cycle of life in order to rise to communion with Eternal God within their soul. Thus, life is mortal, but the spirit is immortal.

Sikhism teaches that after death the body will not remain in the grave until the end of the world. The Day of Judgement will come to every person immediately after their death. It also teaches that heaven and hell are not locations but they are symbolically represented by joy or sorrow, bliss and agony, light and darkness. Hell is seen as a corrective experience in which people suffer in continuous cycles of birth and death. The burden may only be thrown off by living a perfect life.

In Sikhism there are two distinct doctrines about rebirth. Firstly, when the soul passes from one life to another in spiritual progress, nirvana (or perfection) is eventually achieved through reincarnation. Secondly, rebirth in animal life is punishment. In striving for nirvana it is believed that the soul of the Sikh passes through a number of stages and moral conditions. These stages are known as:

1. the region of divine righteousness
2. the region of divine illumination
3. the region of spiritual beauty and modesty
4. the region of grace
5. the region of truth and light of God.

Thus a person is able to conquer death through the discipline of Sikhism, climbing the five steps of the ladder of spiritual effort to immortality.

Death rites

At a Sikh's death bed, friends and relatives read the sukmani (song of peace) to console themselves and to give comfort to the dying person. When death occurs, those present exclaim 'Waheguru!' (wonderful Lord) but loud lamentations are not considered appropriate. The body is washed and dressed. Men are wrapped in a white cotton shroud with a turban. Older women may also be dressed in a white shroud but a younger woman is wrapped in a red shroud or perhaps her red wedding sari. The Five K's (kesh, kangha, kara, kirpan, kaccha) are worn by the deceased and the body is taken home for friends and relatives to pay their last respects before the funeral. Gifts of oil or money may also be put into the coffin.

Cremation will take place as soon as possible after death but the body will normally be taken to the gurdwara (place of worship) first although it is not normally taken into the presence of the Guru Granth Sahib (holy book). In India the body will be cremated on a funeral pyre but elsewhere it may be taken to a crematorium. In either case, arrangements will be made for a close male relative to be present to light the fire. As the fire is lit the Sohila (bed time prayers) are recited, from the Guru Granth Sahib.

The relatives and friends then return to the gurdwara to hear a sermon. A passage about death is read from the holy book and a hymn is offered (the Anand Sahib). A prayer known as the Ardas is recited and the Guru Granth Sahib is opened at random and a verse of guidance (vak) is read out. The service concludes with the distribution of food (karah parshad) which symbolises the continuity of social life and normal activities and the rejection of fasting and grief.

For about ten days after the funeral relatives will gather, either at home or in the gurdwara, for the completion of the reading of the Guru Granth Sahib. Donations to the temple or to a charity are normally given. The bones of the deceased (or ashes) are gathered, and in India they are scattered into a river. Elsewhere they may be flown home to be sprinkled in sacred rivers.

Islam

There are about 1 million Muslims in the United Kingdom. Most Muslim families originate from the Asian sub-continent, the Middle-East, Africa and Turkey. Urdu, Gujerati, Bengali and Arabic may be spoken at home and in the religious community. There has never been any doubt in Islam about life after death. The very first statement of belief declares faith in God, angels, his books and the final resurrection. Death is regarded in the Qur'an as the certainty which cannot be put off. Everyone is subject to death but it is not until the day of resurrection that humankind's reward will be paid in full. It is believed that the souls of the departed are taken into the charge of the Angel of Death and held until the Day of Judgement. This waiting stage is known as Barzakh. On the Day of Judgement Muslims believe that all the dead will be raised and will be held to account before God. On this day there will also be a cosmic upheaval and all the earth and heavens will be destroyed. The Judgement will consist of five stages:

- **The Presentation before Allah.** All people will present themselves. No one will be able to hide their misdeeds.
- **The Books of Account.** Examining angels will have already prepared books in which all good and bad actions are recorded. These books will then be given in the right or left hand of each person to whom they belong. Good deeds will be held in the right hand and bad deeds in the left hand.
- **The Questioning.** Firstly Allah will question the Prophets about the response which each individual has shown towards them. Next humankind will be questioned about their actions, motivations and intentions. These will be taken into account.
- **The Account.** Allah will make each individual aware of the record of their actions. These actions may include injustices towards animals.
- **The Weighing in the Balance.** (Mizah). A balance will be set up in order to weigh good and bad actions.

Final Judgement

After the entire record for every person is laid before Allah, he will consider each case judicially. Those who excel in goodness and pious conduct will receive a reward in Jannah (garden of peace) where they will lead a life of happiness forever. Those whose evil actions and wrongs outweigh their good deeds will be punished and sent to Jahannam (hell), where they will be scorched by eternal fire. There are numerous descriptions concerning Jannah and Jahannam. Generally the garden of peace is seen as having rivers flowing through it and food and wine served by youthful boys. Jahannam is said to be guarded by 19 angels who administer punishment in the fire. Both heaven and hell are seen as everlasting. There is no intermediate state.

Death rites and burial

When death approaches a Muslim is urged to recite the Shahadah 'there is no God except Allah'. If they are able to do so they are also expected to seek forgiveness and mercy from God. Relatives will normally gather by the bedside and read passages from the Qur'an. On hearing of the death, it is usual to say, 'to God we belong, and to Him we return'. Relatives will gather at the home of the deceased comforting the family and praying for God's forgiveness and mercy.

The body is washed three times and covered in a shroud consisting of three pieces of white cloth. Muslims who have performed the Hajj (pilgrimage to Makkah) may have brought back a shroud for their burials. Scent or perfume may be used on the body which is usually buried without delay. It is put on a bier or in a coffin and carried to a mosque or burial ground for funeral prayers. At the place of the service the Imam (spiritual leader) faces Makkah and recites four sayings of Allah before the body is placed in the grave with the head facing Makkah. Some Muslims believe that the grave should be sufficiently deep for the deceased person to sit up on the Day of Judgement. Verses are recited from the Qur'an e.g. 'from the earth did we create you, and into it shall we return you, and from it shall we bring you out once again'.

The grave should be raised slightly above the ground to prevent it being walked on but high gravestones and monuments are forbidden. Mourning is considered natural, but loud wailings are forbidden. Mourning periods vary between seven days and three months and during this time no celebrations will take place in the deceased's family, but visits to the grave are recommended on Eid days (festival days). Some Muslims will visit the grave every Friday for forty days after the death. A widow will traditionally modify her behaviour for about four months, wearing plain clothes, no jewellery, and staying in the house if possible.

The following points are important:

- Post mortem is forbidden except in very special circumstances.
- Prolonging life by artificial means is forbidden.
- Muslims should be buried in a Muslim cemetery.
- Cremation is forbidden.

Hinduism

It is estimated there are between 350,000 to 1 million Hindus in the United Kingdom. The most common languages are Gujarati, Hindi, Punjabi, Tamil and Bengali. In the Indian tradition the life of a person is held to be a pilgrimage from the cradle to the grave. Indian and Far Eastern religions are often said to have a cyclic notion of human life and the universe, teaching that all things move round in cycles of birth, death and rebirth. It is believed that liberation or salvation can be obtained from this cycle or chain of rebirth into the bliss of Nirvana. Belief in rebirth (reincarnation and transmigration) is characteristic of Hinduism and it seems that the notion originated in the ancient philosophical Upanishads (writings) about 800–600 BCE.

In life, the Hindu is said to pass through sixteen stages, or take sixteen steps each of which is dedicated to God through a ritual called Samskara. The first of these takes place before birth and the last takes place after death. The sixteenth is the ceremony of cremation. The Hindu doctrine of Karma teaches that those people who have done good deeds in this life will be born into affluent families, but those whose behaviour had been evil will be born again as outcasts or animals.

Belief in rebirth is based upon the conviction that the soul is immortal and is indestructible. There are many stories in Hinduism about heavens and hells, which may be considered as intermediary places of reward or punishment before rebirth. Different gods have their own heavens, for example on the mythical mountain Meru in the centre of the earth, or in the northern ocean where Vishnu rests on a coiled snake with a thousand heads. Hell is a place of torment called Naraka, divided into either seven or twenty-one levels, and sometimes there are said to be eighty-six pits full of fire and torture.

Death rites and cremation

In the last stages of life a Hindu would wish to spend time in prayer and contemplation of the next life, abstaining from sensual pleasures, leading life in a calm and a detached way. After death contact with a dead body is avoided as much as possible and mourners will avoid contact with outsiders. Before cremation a dead body is washed and then wrapped in a white shroud or white clothes. A young bride may be wrapped in a length of red material. Bodies are usually placed in a coffin and a coin or a small piece of gold or a leaf from the sacred tulsi plant may be placed in the dead person's mouth.

In India the coffin is tied to a funeral pyre which is carried by six mourners to the cremation grounds. The eldest member of the family leads the mourners. In India, ghee (clarified butter) is poured onto the pyre to help the fire catch alight, and the eldest son, or nearest male relation, lights the pyre. Sacred texts are recited by the priest during the cremation, for example 'may your eyesight return to the sun, your breath to the winds: may your water mingle with the ocean and your earthly parts become one with the earth.' The mourners process around the pyre in an anticlockwise direction before either bathing in a river or taking a bath to wash away the spiritual pollution of death.

On the third day after the cremation the ashes are collected and, if possible, they are scattered onto a river, preferably the sacred river Ganges. In the days following the death the whole family is in mourning. Women may not eat until after the cremation has taken place. The widow and eldest son of a deceased man may shave their heads and many members of the family will wear white for ten days after the death. The final ceremony is performed on the eleventh or thirteenth day after the cremation and is known as the kriya ceremony. All who attended the cremation will be present. Offerings of rice-balls and milk are made to the deceased to show gratitude for the kind deeds performed in the life just ended and to help the spirit to its next birth. After this ceremony the mourners are no longer considered to be spiritually impure and they will return to normal living.

In Great Britain Hindus would wish to be cremated. It is quite usual for families to fly the body of the deceased back to the homeland.

Orthodox Judaism

Approximately 300,000 Jews live in the United Kingdom. There are references in the Jewish Bible which show that the ancient Israelites believed in life after death. Graves, especially those of important people, were not only burial places but often became sanctuaries and places of pilgrimage. Phrases in the Bible which speak of a man being 'gathered to his fathers', 'sleeping with his fathers', or being 'laid in the sepulchre with his fathers', suggest that humankind joined their ancestors in the sleep of death. In the Hebrew religion there appeared to be a notion of Sheol, or place of the departed, described as 'the land of darkness' or, 'the land of forgetfulness'. Psalm 88 states, 'my life draws near unto Sheol'.

Jewish teaching has always maintained that speculation on the form which an afterlife takes is somewhat pointless, yet there is a definite belief in an afterlife and in reward and punishment after earthly life. It is true however that the emphasis is upon living a good and righteous life on earth as a preparation for life in the world to come.

Today Orthodox Judaism believes that the soul of a person lives on when the body dies and that at the time of the resurrection when the Messiah comes, it will be reunited with the body. The idea of 'hell' is a little vague, but it is generally interpreted to mean that a person cannot automatically go to 'heaven' if they have led a bad life. Hell is therefore a place of suffering for misdeeds.

Dying

Hastening death is forbidden in Judaism, whatever the circumstances, although the prolonging of life in elderly persons is not seen to be essential.

If a sick person realises that their life is ebbing away, they will endeavour to recite the Viddui or the 'confession of the dead bed'. This is a short Hebrew prayer which acknowledges that life or death are in the hands of God. The prayer also accepts the possibility of death and requests that death should atone for any sins committed during life. Long life is requested for relatives.

It is hoped that the Shema, 'Hear, Israel, the Lord our God is One God' should be the last words of the dying person. This moment of death is referred to as 'the time of departure of the soul'. Judaism believes that the soul ascends to 'a world to come' and that the soul is an integral part of every human being.

Among the main organisations of every Jewish community is the 'Holy Fraternity' (Hebra Kadisha). This is a voluntary group whose task it is to supervise and to carry out all rites and arrangements connected with the death. It is considered an honour to assist in the burial of the dead and a clear relic of this lies in the tradition at the funeral of each person present helping to shovel a little earth onto the grave.

After the departure of the soul, the bodily remains are treated with great respect and the corpse is not left alone by day or night, until the funeral. The funeral will take place as soon as possible after the death. Beforehand the body is washed by members of the Hebra Kadisha, but no embalming is permitted. It is dressed in plain white garments and placed in an unvarnished wooden coffin.

Burial service

The funeral service is brief and simple, designed for the honour and dignity of the deceased. The dominant themes are:

- The recognition of God as the "True Judge".
- The cycle of life.
- An expression of belief in the progress of the soul.

Cremation was traditionally forbidden in Judaism because it is believed that when the Messiah comes the dead will be physically resurrected. However, cremation is increasingly popular among non-practising Jews and among Reform Jews who do not believe in the physical resurrection of the dead.

Grief and mourning

Judaism has evolved a hierarchy of mourning patterns which reflect Jewish attitudes towards death and dying. The first mention of mourning practices among the Israelites can be found in the Bible. In Genesis we read that Reuben tears his garment and Job, in the Book of Job, on hearing of the death of his children, does the same. There are references to the wearing of sackcloth and in the book of Micah the mourner goes naked. Putting dust on the head is common and likewise shaving the head and beard. Although many of these traditions are no longer observed, and in some cases they have been reversed, the principle remains the same – a mourner does the opposite of normal custom in order to show their change of status. The most striking expression of grief today is the tearing of a piece of garment prior to the funeral service.

Judaism believes that it is essential for the bereaved persons to express their grief thoroughly so that they will be able to return to everyday life without having repressed their emotions. A period of mourning also enables members of the community to talk about the bereavement. Indeed, comforting mourners is considered to be one of the primary duties of Judaism.

There are four clearly recognised stages of mourning:

From death to burial

During this time the mourner is exempt from certain religious obligations (e.g. regular prayer) and the main task is arranging the funeral. At the commencement of the funeral, tearing of a lapel is performed. Very orthodox women are usually discouraged from going to the cemetery although they may follow the cortege for a few yards down the street.

The Shiva

For seven days after the funeral close relatives gather daily at the house of mourning. Mourners sit on low chairs and are comforted by family, friends and neighbours. Daily prayers are said for the deceased and mourning patterns are observed. Bereaved persons may not have their hair cut, wear leather shoes, shave, go to work, study the Torah, or prepare food for themselves.

Shaloshim

For 30 days after the funeral, personal mourning is observed. Bereaved persons may go to work but they should avoid shaving and hair cuts, and new clothes or make-up should not be worn. Attending celebrations or listening to music is forbidden, but mourners have the privilege of reciting a piece of liturgy (kaddish) at synagogue services and most Jews would attempt to do this.

Shaloshim to First Yahrzeit

After the initial month of mourning, there are a further 11 months of mourning. Kaddish is said during this time and the mourners still observe certain patterns of mourning. A headstone with a very simple inscription in Hebrew is usually erected and a blessing said over it. The anniversary of death is marked by the reciting of liturgy, the lighting of a memorial candle, and often by performing some act of righteousness, such as making a donation to the synagogue or charity. New born babies are often named after the deceased and a candle may be lit each year on the anniversary of the death. NB Reform and Liberal Jewish communities have amended the rituals of mourning, for example, cremation is permitted and Shiva may not be observed for the full seven days.

Buddhism

Buddhism shares many basic ideas with Hinduism because it emerged in India from the same roots. The religion was revealed by Sitthartha Gautama who lived among men and women sharing direct experience of their problems. He had stepped very close to death but had found within himself resources to deal with the fear, sorrow and pain of mourning, and for forty-five years he worked among humanity helping them to understand that death and life were two phases of one process.

Sometime after the Buddha's death, his followers divided into two groups. The Theravada school of Southern Buddhism is found in Sri Lanka, Burma, Thailand, Laos, and Kampuchea. The Mahayana school originates in Northern Buddhism and is found today in Nepal, Tibet, Bhutan, Japan, Korea and is practised by some Chinese people. Therefore it is not easy to generalise about the main different beliefs and practices of the religion, and funeral rites specific to these two groups will be considered separately. However, most Buddhists believe that humans consist of five elements, all of which are in a state of change.

These elements are:

- The body (rupa)
- Sensation or feeling (vedana)
- Perception or experience of feelings (sanja)
- Impulses (sanskara)
- Consciousness (vijnana)

None of these components is permanent.

Connected with this belief is that of a continuation of life, birth and death in accordance with behaviour. In Buddhism there is no known beginning to life. But the ultimate fate of humanity can be determined by the individual. For most people there is the possibility of many lifetimes of effort before the liberation of nirvana is achieved. The idea of nirvana may have begun with the Buddhists. Nirvana ends suffering and gives security.

Ancient Buddhist stories described heaven as full of beautiful 'beings' wearing perfumed garlands; trees covered with ripe fruits and flowers; birds with brilliant plumage and nymphs in the prime of youth. In contrast hell is ruled by demons who tie up damned persons with ropes, drive hot stakes through them and drag them across blazing fires. The torture of hell is not everlasting however, and when evil transgressions are purged, the soul may rise again to other chances on earth. Similarly heaven is not eternal: when merit is exhausted there are further lives to live until the final attainment and liberation of nirvana.

Death and funeral rites in Theravada Buddhism

Theravada Buddhism is the mainstream and 'strictest' form of Buddhism. Theravada Buddhists do not believe that an individual is reborn but that the energies of good and bad which were created in their lifetime will be incorporated into a new person at birth affecting his or her life. The funeral ceremony has become an opportunity to honour the deceased and also to gain spiritual merit for the living and the dead, through the giving of gifts to monks. Funerals in Theravada Buddhism are much more elaborate than those found in Mahayana Buddhism. Funeral carriages are richly decorated and caskets are surrounded by flowers and gifts. A photograph of the deceased is usually placed near the casket to remind those present of the transient nature of life.

When the family are assembled the monk who has been invited to conduct the ceremony will lead the congregation in the traditional declaration of respect for the Buddha known as Three Refuges or Jewels:

- I go for refuge to the Buddha
- I go for refuge to the Dharma
- I go for refuge to the Sangha

This is followed by the recitation of The Five Precepts or The Five Promises made by Buddhists, to refrain from:

- Harming living creatures
- Taking what is not given
- Misuse of the physical senses
- Speaking falsely
- Using intoxicating drinks or drugs

A sermon is then delivered on the subject of impermanence. Throughout the ceremony food is prepared, musical instruments are played and the atmosphere is one of a festive occasion, with the emphasis not on death, but on new life. Crying and other forms of grief are rarely shown. After the service the body is cremated and the remains are either buried in a graveyard or kept in a temple in a small urn.

Death and funeral rites in Mahayana Buddhism

Mahayana Buddhism arose as another strand of Buddhism. Mahayana Buddhism welcomes into its fabric the beliefs and practices of other religious systems and there are as many philosophies and beliefs as there are groups of people who practise it. Funeral rites are less elaborate than in Theravada Buddhism but the two groups use cremation services which are similar in form.

The day on which death occurs is considered to be very important and it is believed that the personality of the deceased remains in a state of trance for four days. This is known as First Bardo and it is the time when the deceased may be reached through the spiritual power of monks. Towards the end of this phase it is said that the person sees a brilliant light. If he or she is able to tolerate the light then rebirth will not take place, but most people flee from the light. At the Second Bardo the deceased sees all his or her past thoughts and deeds passing before them. Then comes the Third Bardo which is the state of seeking rebirth when the deceased chooses new parents, who give them their next body.

Chinese religions

Chinese people in the United Kingdom come mostly from Hong Kong, Malaysia, Singapore, Taiwan and Vietnam. Chinese written language comprises over 16,000 thousand characters, each character representing a word. The official language of China is Mandarin although in the UK Hakka and Cantonese are more commonly used. Chinese religion embraces Buddhism, Confucianism and Toaism. Therefore it is difficult to be definitive about Chinese belief and practice. However, many of the practices associated with death and mourning rites are not dissimilar from those within mainstream Buddhism. Many Chinese families would wish for the following around the time of death:

- For the dying person to have the company of somebody of the same culture and religious tradition.
- For the body of the dead person to be dressed in white and for mourners to wear white.
- For family members to be given time to travel to the funeral.
- For burial to be with other Chinese people or where cremation takes place, to bury or scatter the ashes in a place set aside for members of the Chinese community.

Whilst it is dangerous to generalise about how people experiencing bereavement would wish others to respond to them, most religious communities would welcome:

- people who give sufficient space and time to carry out what needs to be done (either emotionally or religiously);
- people who are 'safe' to be with and who know sufficient about religious belief and practice to be sensitive to the needs and requirements of the family.

Rites and rituals surrounding death

The following section attempts to summarise the practices and attitudes towards death of the various religions discussed in this chapter.

Sensitivities which should be shown to families

For those people with a strong religious conviction the meaning of life and the meaning of death are inextricably bound. In many faiths life is a preparation for death and the life to come. It is extremely difficult to summarise the most common rituals and ceremonies which occur at the time of death or immediately afterwards. This section attempts to raise awareness of some of the sensitivities which should be shown towards families.

Christianity
- The dying person may wish to receive Holy Communion and/or The Sacrament of the Sick (or Sacrament of Reconciliation).
- The family may wish to say prayers thanking God for the life of the person and the life to come.
- Prayers may be said on behalf of the family and on behalf of the dying person.
- A quiet place will be appreciated in order for the family to pray or to talk with a priest or minister.
- The family will want to carry out the wishes of the dead person and to be able to make their own decisions with regard to burial or cremation. In some traditions Mass or Communion may be included in the funeral service.

Judaism
- It is usual for someone to be with the person at the time of death. Some Jews would wish for a rabbi to be present.
- Shema is said either by the person who is dying or by the relatives (the declaration of faith).
- The body is washed by members of the Jewish community (Orthodox).
- In the Orthodox tradition physical contact with the body will be avoided by members of the opposite sex.
- The body will be accompanied from the time of death to time of burial.
- The body will be buried as soon as possible after death, preferably within 25 hours (but not on the Sabbath or holy days).
- In Orthodox communities close family members will mourn for a period of 30 days after the death.
- In Orthodox communities close family members will refrain from attending celebrations for the period of mourning.
- At the end of the period of mourning a tombstone will be consecrated with a ceremony at the cemetery.

Islam
- If possible, the declaration of faith (Shahada) will be recited before death.
- A dying person will wish to have somebody with them.
- Family members will try to be together where possible.
- Post mortems will not take place except where demanded by civil law.
- The dead body will be washed three times and dressed in clean clothes. Family members will wish to wash themselves afterwards.

- The head of the deceased is turned onto the right shoulder and then positioned facing Makkah (south-east in the UK).
- The body is covered with a plain clean cloth.
- The next of kin will make the funeral arrangements. Islamic law requires friends and relations to feed mourners for three days after the death.
- Burial will take place as soon as possible and cremation will be forbidden.
- The body may be returned to the place of birth. In some cases the body may be embalmed.
- Apart from blood relatives the mourners will avoid bodily contact with persons of the opposite sex.
- Relatives may wish to visit the grave regularly on Fridays for up to 40 days after the death. Mourning ends with a meal and Qur'anic reading.
- Families will appreciate being provided with accommodation in a non-smoking and alcohol-free place.

Hinduism
- The dying person will wish to have someone with them. They may wish to lie on the floor and to sip Holy Ganges' water.
- The body will be washed after death by members of the religious community.
- The body will be wrapped in a white shroud or white clothes, except in the case of a young woman, who may be wrapped in a red sari.
- A gold coin or leaf from the sacred tulsi plant may be put in the mouth of the deceased person.
- Family members will wish to keep the body close to them or as close to the Hindu community as possible.
- There should be an opportunity for the family to talk to other family members or somebody from the religious community (they may prefer somebody of the same sex as themselves).
- The next of kin will wish to make the funeral arrangements. The first part of the ceremony may take place at home.
- The body will be cremated with the exception of children under three years old who will be buried.
- The eldest male in the family will play a key role in the funeral service.
- In India a period of 10–16 days is spent mourning. In Great Britain there may be rituals during the first year after death.

Sikhism
- Sikhs will wish to have somebody with them at the time of their death. They may wish to have portions of the Guru Granth Sahib read to them.

- After death the body will be washed before cremation and dressed by members of the family or members of the religious community.
- Sikhs will wish to wear the five Ks wherever possible, including a white turban for a man. Young women will be dressed in a red sari or a red shroud.
- The body will be covered with a clean white sheet and money or other gifts may be placed in the coffin.
- Sikhs will wish other people from outside their community to refrain from comforting them or having physical contact with them e.g. hugging.
- Families may like to listen to readings from the Guru Granth Sahib for about ten days after the funeral.
- Families will appreciate being provided with accommodation in a non-smoking and alcohol-free environment.
- If the father of the family has died the eldest son may be given a turban to signify he is now head of the family.

Buddhism
- Where possible, families will wish to be with the person who is dying. A religious teacher may be invited to talk to the person.
- The body will remain untouched until a priest arrives.
- Family members will stay together for as long as possible.
- The body will be washed after death and laid out, sometimes by members of the family or religious community.
- An environment will be appreciated which is as quiet as possible and conducive to prayer/ meditation.
- A photograph of the deceased may be placed near the coffin.
- A period of between three and seven days will usually elapse before the funeral.
- Burial or cremation will depend on the school of Buddhism/country of origin.
- Periods of mourning vary according to the country of origin.

Glossary of Terms

This glossary attempts to explain some of the more complex terms used by professionals who care for people at the time of death, or for their families. Words used by religious communities are covered in Chapter 9, Death in World Religions, and they are explained within the main body of the text as appropriate.

Bier	Support for a coffin, wheeled or fixed
Body Bag	A waterproof bag, with or without handles in which to hold the deceased
Bereavement	The loss by death of someone
Cadaver	A medical term for a corpse
Catafalque	Support for a coffin, normally used in a crematorium during the service
Catacomb	Underground cemetery or cellar
Cenotaph	Tomblike monument, especially a war memorial, for a person whose body is elsewhere
Chapel of Rest	A room in which the deceased is lain for viewing
Committal	Part of the funeral service when the remains are committed to the elements
Coroner	The person responsible for enquiry into sudden, violent or unnatural death
Coroner's Officer	The person who deals with the administration of an enquiry
Corpse	The dead body
Cremation	Disposal of the body by burning, reducing it to ashes
Cryonics	The freezing of a body with a view to it being defrosted and resuscitated in the future when technology is suitably advanced
Disbursement	Cost of services arranged by a funeral director on behalf of a client
Encephalograph	A machine which traces the electric impulses in the brain
Embalming	Injection of fluids into the body to enhance the appearance, reduce danger of infection and temporarily preserve remains

Euthanasia	The bringing about of a gentle and easy death in the case of incurable and painful disease
Executor	Male person appointed by the deceased to carry out the provisions of his or her will
Executrix	Female executor
Exequies	Funeral rites
Exhumation	Removal of dead body from the grave or another resting place
Family Tomb	A large underground vault for the burial of members of the same family
First Offices/Last Offices	Care of deceased carried out by the funeral director including washing and dressing
Flat Line	The reading on an encephalograph which indicates brain death
Funeral Director	The director and manager of the service arrangements for dealing with the deceased
Funeral Home	The buildings containing the offices and facilities for preparing the deceased for burial or cremation
Furnace	The oven in the crematorium
Hades	Greek: the underworld, the abode of spirits of the dead
Heaven	A place regarded in some religions as the abode of God, and of good persons after death
Hell	A place regarded in some religions as the abode of the dead, or of condemned sinners
Last Rites	Sacred rites for a person about to die
Liturgy	The book of common prayer
Mausoleum	Large grave or tomb
Memorial	A gravestone
Near Death Experience	The sense of leaving one's body and glimpsing some other existence
Necrology	A list of recently dead people, and obituary notice
Necrophobia	Abnormal fear of death or dead bodies
Neo-natal Death	Death of a child within four weeks of birth
Obsequies	Funeral rites
Ossuary	A receptacle for bones of the dead
Post Mortem	Examination made after death
Psyche	The soul, the spirit
Reincarnation	The rebirth of the soul into a new body
Relics	The dead body or remains of a person
Reliquary	Receptacle for relics
Sepulchre	A tomb especially cut in rock or built in stone or brick
Side-sets	Decorative linings for the sides of the coffin interior
Will	A document containing directions for the disposition of one's property after death.

Picture Story Books

Early Years, Key Stage 1

Burningham, J. (1988) *Granpa*. London: Puffin. A beautiful picture book which tells about the death of a little girl's grandfather.

Carle, E. (1994) *The Very Hungry Caterpillar*. London: Puffin. A story which tells the life-cycle of the caterpillar. The book has potential for discussion about death and resurrection.

Curtis-Stilz, C. (1988) *Kirsty's Kite*. Tring: Albatross. Kirsty's mother has died, leaving her in the care of her granddad. Kirsty longs to be with her mother again and as she flies her kite and talks to her granddad she begins to understand that although her mother is in heaven, her special memories live on for ever.

Dale, E. (1996) *Scrumpy*. London: Anderson Press. A tale about a much loved pet dog called Scrumpy who becomes ill and dies. Ben, his young owner, is terribly upset and the illustrations show him crying.

Eachus, J. (1994) *The Big Big Sea*. London: Walker Books. A beautifully illustrated book which tells of special relationships which can never be forgotten.

Egger, B. (1987) *Mary and Her Grandmother*. New York: Viking Penguin. When Mary's grandmother dies, Mary remembers all the things that she shared. Mary realises she still lives in her even though she will never see her again.

Girard, L. and Sims, B. (1991) *Alex, the Kid with AIDS*. New York: Whitman. Alex feels anxious and confused that he has AIDS. He also feels excluded by his peers. Gradually Alex begins to accept himself and his friends are helped to accept him too.

Hayes, S., and Craig, H. (1991) *This is the Bear and the Scary Night*. London: Walker Books. A young boy feels frightened and lost in the dark. Through telling the story of how his teddy got lost and spent a night alone in the park, he begins to talk about his fears.

Isherwood, S. (1996) *My Grandad*. Oxford: Oxford University Press. A book about memories and special shared times between a little girl and her grandfather. Lavishly illustrated.

Krisher, T. (1992) *Kathy's Hats*. New York: Whitman. Kathy has loved hats since she was a very little girl but when she develops cancer and she has a course of chemotherapy her hair falls out and she discovers she hates wearing a hat. With her mum's help she learns to accept how she looks and to think about hats in a better light.

Lanton, S. (1991) *Daddy's Chair*. Rockville, USA: Kar-Ben Copies. A book about a Jewish family which describes mourning customs within the Jewish tradition. Michael is very possessive of his Daddy's chair and he remembers how before he died it was a special place where they shared special times together.

Limb, S. (1995) *Come Back, Grandma*. London: Red Fox. Bessie loves her grandmother. When her mum and dad were busy, her grandma always had time for her. A simple story of memories with delightful pictures.

Mansell, D. (1993) *My Old Teddy*. London: Walker Books. When toys and people get old their bodies wear out. A little girl's teddy begins to fall apart but it doesn't really matter because nothing can replace the love and the relationship which has developed over the years.

Maple, M. (1992) *On the Wings of a Butterfly – a story about life and death*. Seattle: Parenting Press. A gentle, honest story about a little girl called Lisa dying of cancer, who finds comfort and support in her friendship with a caterpillar, preparing for metamorphosis into a beautiful butterfly. The two share their fears and questions and embrace the unknown together.

Simmonds, P. (1989) *Fred*. London: Puffin. Nick and Sophie's old cat Fred dies. The children bury him at the end of the garden. An ideal book for talking about the death of a pet and for helping to explain funerals.

Techner, D. and Hirt-Manheimer, J. (1993) *A Candle for Grandpa*. New York: UAHC Press. A story which introduces children to traditional Orthodox Jewish funerals. The narrative tells of how a family grieves but how the religious tradition helps during the sadness.

Varley, S. (1994) *Badger's Parting Gifts*. London: Picture Lions. When old Badger dies, his friends think they will be sad for ever. But gradually they are able to remember him with joy and gratitude and to treasure the gifts he left behind for each one of them. A sensitively written, highly acclaimed book which helps children come to terms with the death of someone they love.

Williams, M. (1988) *The Velveteen Rabbit*. London: Heinemann. A beloved, battered toy rabbit is burnt on the bonfire when his owner gets scarlet fever. A delightful story set in a Victorian nursery which explores children's views of the survival of the spirit.

Wolf, W. and Alison, J. (1994) *Christmas with Grandfather*. London: North South Books. After his father was killed in an accident Thomas finds he cannot believe in Christmas any longer. When his grandfather invites him to spend Christmas in the house where his dad grew up, Thomas begins to come to terms with what has happened and the sadness he has felt.

Key Stage 2

Ashley, B. (1991) *Seeing Off Uncle Jack*. London: Viking. A realistic book which contains two stories about how a family cope with bereavement in a way which remembers both the endearing and the less loveable sides of Uncle Jack's character.

Hamilton, V. (1990) *Cousins*. London: Gollancz. A story about rivalry and jealousy between friends with a theme of making and breaking relationships, forgiveness and reconciliation after the accidental drowning of a young child.

Jordon, M. (1989) *Losing Uncle Tim*. New York: Whitman. An honest and moving tale about a young man called Uncle Tim who has AIDS. Sensitively written with good illustrations which lend themselves to discussions about feelings including prejudice and compassion.

Kaldhol, M. (1987) *Goodbye Rune*. New York: Miller. A story which describes how young friends respond to the accidental drowning of Rune. The text answers many of the questions which children will ask, such as whether a dead person still thinks and grows, and it is an excellent book for helping children to grow through their own grief of tragic death.

Lee, V. (1983) *The Magic Moth*. London: Langman. Ten year old Maryanne is life-threatened with heart disease and her younger brother is confused about why she doesn't get any better. An honest and practical story about a family's grief which ends with Maryanne's death marked by a moth which flies out of the window. The moth becomes a symbol for Maryanne's brother Mark-O which sustains him throughout the funeral and beyond.

Madenski, M. and Ray, D. (1991) *Some of the Pieces*. London: Little Brown. Young Dylan's father died and was cremated. However his memory is kept alive by his family who scatter his ashes in places where they remember the good times they shared with him.

Mayfield, S. (1990) *I Carried You On Eagle's Wings*. London: AD Library. A young mother has been diagnosed with multiple sclerosis before the birth of her son Tony. A story which describes the grief of a family when a member is life-threatened and then dies. The importance of grieving is lived out by Tony and his father at the time of death, the funeral and in the time afterwards.

Morpurgo, M. (1987) *Conker*. London: Heinemann. A young boy, who is cared for by his grandmother, experiences the death of his pet dog Conker. A moving story which endorses the idea that the cost of loving is the pain of loss through bereavement.

Piumini, R. (1993) *Mattie and Grandpa*. London: Puffin. A moving story which describes the stresses and anxiety of a family who are aware Grandpa is dying in hospital. As the family sit around his bed they share what it feels like to enter in to the intimate experience of watching someone die.

Rees, S. (1992) *Saturdays, Playdays and Other Days*. London: Rebec Press. A unique and honest story about the loss of a baby through miscarriage and how Emma and Catrin aged seven cope when Catrin's mum is in hospital and she stays with her friend Emma.

Sims, A. (1986) *Am I Still a Sister?* New York: A & C Co. Alicia is eleven when her baby brother dies of a brain tumour. Alicia writes her thoughts and memories down in letters written to Austin after his death. This is a superb book for helping children to understand what it is like to grieve.

White, E. B. (1963) *Charlotte's Web*. London: Puffin. A classic well-loved story about a farmer's daughter called Fern who cares for a piglet who befriends a spider called Charlotte. As the story unfolds the piglet learns about life experiences including mortality.

Key Stage 3

Ashton, J. (1995) *Killing the Demons*. London: Puffin. Samantha survives a road traffic accident in which her brother dies, but she has sustained bad injuries and will be confined to a wheelchair. She does not believe that life will be worth living again but after she moves to Wales and makes new friends her quality of life begins to improve.

Duder, T. (1990) *Alex*. London: Penguin. Like most teenagers Alex is sometimes rebellious and difficult to understand. When her boyfriend sustains fatal injuries after being hit by a car which fails to stop, she discovers that managing her own emotions and taking responsibility for them is a very grown up thing to do.

Henkes, K. (1995) *Words of Stone*. London: Red Fox. Blaze cannot remember his mother because she died when he was a baby. He grows up with his father and his grandmother and has always been frightened of confronting or expressing his feelings. Joselle is a special friend who helps him to reflect on who he really is and to accept his emotions.

Hill, D. (1995) *See ya, Simon*. London: Puffin. Simon is life-limited because he is coping with the advanced stages of muscular dystrophy. His friend Nathan is determined he will make the very best of the life which he has left and the two lads get up to some amazing pranks and come to value the meaning of loyalty and friendship.

Hughes, B. (1992) *Then and Now*. Birmingham: Women's Press. Soon after Felicity's father dies in the Falklands war, her mother remarries. The story tells of the love of a young daughter for her dead father and the conflicting emotions which she feels when her mother becomes pregnant. An excellent, moving story.

Mahy, M. (1995) *Memory*. London: Puffin. A powerful tale about Jonny whose sister dies and how he sets out to find her best friend Bonny whom he believes will be able to tell him a great deal about the person he misses so much. As he searches for Bonny and tries to capture the memories of his sister he encounters Sophie who has Alzheimer's disease. Sophie and Jonny become friends and discover they have a lot in common.

Nystrom, C. (1996) *Emma Says Goodbye*. Oxford: Lion. Gill's family are Christian. When her aunt who has terminal cancer comes to live in her home, Gill finds she is angry with God and confused about things like death and suffering. An excellent story with a real-life storyline.

Strachan, I. (1994) *The Boy in the Bubble*. London: Mammoth. Adam has severe combined immunodeficiency and because he is at risk of infection he lives his life in a sterile bubble. A powerful novel with a sensitive but realistic message.

Useful Addresses

ACT
St Michael's Hill
Bristol
BS2 8DZ
Tel. 0117 9221556

Action for Sick Children
Argle House
29–31 Euston Road
London
NW1 2SD
Tel. 0171 8332041

AFTERMATH
PO Box 414
Sheffield
S4 7RT
Tel./Fax 0114 275 8520

ARC (Antinatal Results and Choices).
Was the The Stillbirth and Neonatal Death
Society (SATFA)
73 Charlotte Street
London
W1P 1LB
Tel. 0171 436 7940 (Admin)
0171 436 5881 (Helpline)

BACUP
3 Bath Place
Rivington Street
London
EC2A 3DR
Tel. 0171 613 2121

The Bourne Trust
Lincoln House
Kennington Park
1–3 Brixton Road
London
SW9 6DE

Tel. 0171 582 6699

British Association for Counselling
1 Regents Close
Rugby
Warwickshire
CV21 2PJ
Tel. 01788 578 328 (Information service)
01788 550 899 (Admin)

**British Humanist Association
(Bereavement)**
47 Theobald's Road
London
WC1X 8SP
Tel. 0171 430 0908

Cancer Help Centre
Grove House
Cornwallis Grove
Clifton
Bristol BS8 4PG
Tel. 0117 9809500

Cancer Link
11–21 Northdown Street
London
N1 9BN
Tel. 0171 833 2818

Chai-Lifeline
(Was Jewish Cancer Support Group/Chai-
Lifeline)
Norwood House
Harmony Way
Hendon
NW4 2BZ
Tel. 0181 202 2211
Helpline Tel No. 0181 202 4567

Care Concern
c/o League of Jewish Women
24–32 Stephenson's Way
London
NW1 2JW
Tel. 0181 446 5418
This is a c/o address for Care Concern
because they are moving offices soon.

The Child Bereavement Trust
1 Millside
Riversdale
Bourne End
Bucks
SL8 5EB

The Child Death Helpline
Freephone 0800 282986

CHILDLINE
Freepost 1111
London
N1 0BR
Tel. 0800 1111 (Free helpline for children)
0171 239 1000 (Office)

Compassionate Friends
53 North Street
Bristol
BS3 1EN
Tel. 0117 9665202

Contact a Family
Tel. 0171 383 3555

**Cot Death Research and Support Group
for Bereaved Parents**
14 Halkin Street
London
SW1X 7DP
Tel. 0171 235 0965

Cruse Bereavement Care
126 Sheen Road
Richmond
TW9 1UR
Tel. 0181 940 4818

CSSE (Centre for the Study of Special
Education)
Westminster College

Harcourt Hill
Oxford
OX2 9AT
Tel. 01865 253319

Federation of Prisoner's Families
Support Groups (FPFSG)
c/o SCF
Cambridge House
Cambridge Grove
London
W6 0LE
Tel. 0181 741 4578

**Foundation for the Study of Infant
Deaths.**
14 Halkin St
London
SW1X 7DP
Tel. 0171 235 0965
This is same address and number as for
**Cot Death Research and Support Group
for Bereaved Parents**

Great Ormond Street
Tel. 0171 4059200
**GOS and Alder Hey Hospital, Liverpool
help run a national helpline called Child
Death Helpline,** Tel. 0800 282986
Evenings 7–10pm
Mon/Wed/Fri 10 am–1 pm

Jewish Baby Bereavement Support
Tel. nos. unobtainable.

**The Jewish Bereavement Counselling
Service**
PO Box 6748
London
N3 3BX
Tel. 0181 349 0839

London City Mission
(Was London Bereavement Projects Group)
175 Tower Bridge Road
London
SE1 2AH
Tel. 0171 407 7585

Macmillan Cancer Relief
Anchor House
15–19 Britten Street
London
SW3 3TZ
Tel. 0171 351 7811

Medical Foundation for the Care of Victims of Torture
96–98 Grafton Road
London
NW5 3EJ
Tel. 0171 284 4321

Mi Yad – Jewish Crisis Line
Tel. 0181 203 6211
OPEN Sunday–Thursday 12 noon to midnight
Friday–12–2.00 pm, Saturday–1 hour after Shabbat. Answering service at other times.

The Miscarriage Association
c/o Clayton Hospital
Northgate
Wakefield
W. Yorkshire
WF1 3JS
Tel. 01924 200799

Multiple Birth Foundation
Queen Charlottes and Chelsea Hospital
Goldhawk Road
London
W6 0XG
Tel. 0181 383 3519

National Association for Sick Children
St Margaret's House
17 Old Ford Road
Bethnal Green
London
E2 9PL
Tel. 0181 980 8523

Parent Line
Tel. 01702 554782 (Admin)
Tel. 01702 559900 (Helpline)

Parents Anonymous
Tel. 0171 263 8918
Telephone helpline for parents. 24 hr answerphone.

The Refugee Council
3 Bondway
London
SW8 1SJ
Tel. 0171 582 6922

The Samaritans
Gen office:
10 The Grove
Slough
SL1 1QP
Tel. 01753 532713

The Scottish Cot Death Trust
c/o The Royal Hospital for Sick Children
Yorkhill
Glasgow
Strathclyde
G3 8SJ
Tel. 0141 357 3946

The Stillbirth and Neonatal Death Society (SANDS)
28 Portland Place
London
W1N 4DE
Tel. 0171 436 7940 (Admin)
0171 436 5881 (Helpline)

TAMBA
Twins and Multiple Birth Association
Harnott House
309 Chester Road
Little Sutton
L66 1QQ
Tel. 0151 348 0020

Bibliography

Abrams, R. (1992) *When Parents Die*. London: Letts.

Ahrons, C. and Bowman, M. (1982) 'Changes in family relationships following the divorce of an adult child – grandmothers' perceptions' *Journal of Divorce* **5**, 49–68.

Almond, B., Buckman, W. and Gofman, H. (1979) *The Family is the Patient – an Approach to Behavioural Paediatrics*. London: Mosby.

Amera, Y. (1992) 'We are not the problem: black children and their families within the criminal justice system', in Shaw, R. (ed.) *Prisoners' Children: What are the Issues?* London: Routledge.

Anthony, S. (1973) *The Discovery of Death in Childhood and After*. Harmondsworth: Penguin.

Atkinson, N. and Crawford, M. (1995) *All in the Family: Siblings and Disability*. London: National Children's Homes.

Ayalon, O. and Flasher, A. (1993) *Chain Reaction – Children and Divorce*. London: Jessica Kingsley.

Barnett, W. S. and Boyce, G. C. (1995) 'Effects of Children with Down's Syndrome on parents' activities', *American Journal of Mental Retardation*, **100** (2), 115–27.

Barraclough, B. and Hughes, J. (1987) *Suicide: Clinical and Epidemiological Studies*. London: Croom Helm.

Beckman, P. J. and Beckman-Boyes, G. (eds) (1993) *Deciphering the System: A Guide for Families of Young Children with Disabilities*. Cambridge: M.A. Brookline.

Bending, M. (1993) *Caring for Bereaved Children*. Richmond: CRUSE Bereavement Care.

Bergen, M. (1958) 'Effect of severe trauma on a 4-year-old child'. *Psychoanalytic Study of the Child*, **13**, 407–29.

Berman, W. (1988) 'The role of attachment in the post divorce experience', *Journal of Personality and Social Psychology* **1** (3) 496–503.

Berren, M. R., Beigel, A. and Barker, G. (1982) 'A Typology for the Classification of Disasters: Implications for Intervention', *Community Mental Health Journal* **18** (2), 120–34.

Bihm, E. and Elliot, I. (1982) 'Conception of death in mentally retarded persons', *Journal of Psychology* **3**, 205–10.

Blacher, J. (1984) 'Sequential stages of parental adjustment to the birth of a child with handicaps: fact or artifact?' *Mental Retardation*, **22** (2) 55–68.

Black, D. (1989) 'Life Threatening Illness, Children and Family Therapy', *Journal of Family Therapy*, **22**, 18–24.

Black, D. (1993), untitled in B. Ward and Associates. *Good Grief – Exploring Feelings, Loss and Death* (Vol. 1). London: Jessica Kingsley.

Black, D. and Urbanowicz, M. A. (1987) 'Family intervention with bereaved children', *Journal of Child Psychology and Psychiatry*, **28**, 467–76.

Black, D. and Wood, D. (1989) 'Family therapy and life-threatening illness in children or parents', *Palliative Medicine*, **3**, 113–18.

Blake, J. (1991) *Sentenced by Association*. London: Save the Children.

Bluebond-Langner, M. (1989) 'Worlds of Dying Children and their Well Siblings', *Death Studies* **13**, 1–16.

Bluebond-Langner, M. (1995) *Worlds of Dying Children and their Well Siblings*. in K. Doka (ed.) *Children Mourning, Mourning Children*. Washington: Hospice Association of America.

Bolin, R. C. (1982) *Long-term Family Recovery from Disaster*, Monograph No: 36. University of Colorado: Institute of Behavioural Science.

Bowlby, J. (1969) *Attachment and Loss* (Vol. 1). New York: Basic Books.

Bowlby, J. (1977) *Sadness and Depression; Attachment and Loss*. Harmondsworth: Penguin.

Bradshaw, J. (1990), *Child Poverty and Deprivation in the UK*. London: National Children's Bureau.

Bray, A. (1997) *Fathers and Children with Disabilities*, Seminar at Westminster College, Oxford.

Brelstaff, K. (1984) 'Reactions to death: Can the mentally handicapped grieve? Some experiences of those who did', *Teaching and Training* **22** (1), 10–16.

Brotherson, M. J., Turnbull, A. P., Summers, J. A. and Turnbull, H. R. (1986) 'Fathers of Disabled Children', in Robinson, B. E. and Barrett, R. L. (eds) *The Developing Father*. New York: Guildford, 193–217.

Brown, E. (1993) *The Experiences of Twelve Families with a Child with Profound and Multiple Learning Difficulties*. Unpublished research.

Brown, E. (1994) *Children, Death and Grief*. MA dissertation, Oxford (unpublished).

Brown, E. (1997) *Godparents for 'special' children and their families*, Unpublished paper, Bristol Diocesan Conference, Bristol, February.

Brown, E. (1998) *A Sense of Loss*, Special! Spring 1998, Hobsons Publishers.

Brown, G. and Harris, T. (1989) *Social Origins of Depression*, London: Tavistock.

Brown, J. (1961) *Freud and the Post-Freudians*. Harmondsworth: Pelican Books.

Buckman, R. (1988) *I don't know what to say – How to help and support someone who is dying*. London: Macmillan Paperbacks.

Cadale, D. (1991) *Parenthood Training for Young Offenders: an evaluation of courses in young offenders' institutions*, RFU Paper 63. London: HMSO.

Campion, J. (1991) *Counselling Children*. London: Whiting and Birch.

Caplan, G. (1968) *An Approach to Community Mental Health*. New York: Crune Stratton.

Carpenter, B. and Herbert, E. (1994) 'The peripheral parent: research issues and reflections on the role of fathers in early intervention'. *PMLD Link* (Summer), **19**.

Casale, S. (1989), *Women Inside: The Experience of Women Remand Prisoners in Holloway*. London: Civil Liberties Trust.

Catan, L. (1989a) *The Development of Young Children in HMP Mother and Baby Units*. Occasional Paper in the Social Sciences No.1, Falmer: University of Sussex.

Catan, L. (1989b) *Young Families of Female Prisoners*, Unpublished paper, University of Sussex.

Catan, L. (1992) 'Infants with Mothers in Prison', in Shaw, R. (ed.) *Prisoners' Children: what are the issues?* London: Routledge.

Challella, M. S. (1981) 'Helping Parents Cope with a Profoundly Mentally Retarded Child', in Milansky, A. *Coping with Crisis and Handicap*. New York: Plenum.

Children's Rights Development Unit (1994), *U.K. Agenda for Children*. London: Children's Rights Development Unit.

Chodorow, N. (1990) *Gender, relation and difference in psychoanalytic perspectives*. New York: New York University Press.

Collick, E. (1985) *Through Grief: The Bereavement Journey*. London: Darton, Longman and Todd.

Cooklin, S. (1989) *From Arrest to Release: the inside/outside Survival Guide*. London: Bedford Square Press.

Couldrick, A. (1991) *Grief and Bereavement: Understanding Children*. Oxford: Sobell Publications.

Culling, J. A. (1988) 'The psychological problems of families of children', in Oakhill, A. (ed.) *The Supportive Care of the Child with Cancer*. Bristol: John Wright.

Darling, R. (1993) 'Initial and Continuing Adaption to the Birth of a Disabled Child', in Seligman, M. (ed.) *The Family with a Handicapped Child*. Boston: Allyn and Bacon.

Davis, G. and Murch, M. (1992) *Grounds for Divorce*. Oxford: Clarendon Press.

Department of Health (1989) *The Care of Children: Principles and Practice in Regulations and Guidance*. London: HMSO.

DES (1991) *The Children Act 1989: A Guide for the Education Service*. Milton Keynes: Open University Press.

Dickens, C. (1846) *The Adventures of Oliver Twist*. London: Bradbury and Ebbens.

Doka, K. (ed.) (1993) *Children Mourning, Mourning Children*. Washington: Hospice Association of America.

Duffy, C. (1997) *Palliative Care for Children – a Feasibility Study*, in Papdatou, D. and Papados, C. (eds) *Children and Death*. New York: Hemisphere Books.

Duffy, W. (1991) *The Bereaved Child*. Ongar: The National Society.

Dyregrov, A. (1988) 'Responding to Traumatic Stress Situations in Europe', *Bereavement Care* **4**, 6–9.

Dyregrov, A. (1991) *Grief in Children – A Handbook for Adults*. London: Jessica Kingsley.

Easson, W. (1970) *The Dying Child*. Illinois: Charles Thomas.

Engel, G. L. (1961) 'Is grief a disease? A challenge for medical research', *Psychosomatic Medicine*, **23**, 18–22.

Erickson, P., Drabek, T. E., Key, W. H. and Crowe, J. L. (1976) 'Families in disaster: patterns of recovery', *Mass Emergencies 1*: 203–16.

Eth, S. and Pynoos, R. S. (1985) 'Development perspective on psychic trauma in childhood', in Figley, C. R. (ed.) *Trauma and its Wake*. New York: Brunner Mazel.

Faulkner, A., Peace, G. and O'Keefe, C. (1995) *When a Child has Cancer*. London: Chapman and Hall.

Fewell, R. R. and Meyer, P. F. (eds) (1986) *Families of Handicapped Children*. Austin TX: Pro Ed.

French, J. and Kuczaj, E. (1992) *Working Through Loss and Change with People with Learning Difficulties*, Vol. 20, 108–11.

Freud, S. (1917) *The Standard Edition of the Complete Psychological Works of Sigmund Freud* (Vol. IV). New York: Hogarth Press.

Gascoigne, E. (1995) *Working with Parents as Partners in SEN: Home and School – A Working Alliance*. London: David Fulton Publishers.

Gatliffe, E. (1988) *Death in the Classroom – A Resource Book for Teachers and Others*. London: Epworth.

Geldard, K. and Geldard, D. (1997) *Counselling Children – A Practical Introduction*. London: Sage.

George, J. (1988) 'Therapeutic intervention for grandparents and extended family members of children with developmental delays', *Mental Retardation*, **26**, 369–75.

Goate, A. M. (1991) 'Molecular genetics of Alzheimer's disease', in O'Neill, D. (ed.) *Carers, Professionals and Alzheimer's Disease*, proceedings of the fifth Alzheimer's Disease International Conference, 1989. London: John Libbey.

Graham, N. (1991) 'The Silent Epidemic – who cares?', in O'Neill, D. (ed.) *Carers, Professionals and Alzheimer's Disease*, proceedings of the fifth Alzheimers Disease International Conference, 1989. London: John Libbey.

Harris-Hendricks, J., Black, D. and Kaplan, T. (1993) *When Father Kills Mother*. London: Routledge.

Hautamäki, A. (1997) 'The post-modern family – the interaction between the home and the school', in R. Jakku-Sihvonen (ed.), *Evaluating the Quality of Teaching and Learning*. Helsinki: Finnish Board of Education.

Herbert, M. (1991) *Clinical Child Psychology: Social Learning, Behaviour and Development*. Chichester: J. Wiley.

Herbert, M. (1996) *Supporting Bereaved and Dying Children and their Parents*. Leicester: The British Psychological Society.

Hertfordshire Agreed Syllabus for Religious Education (1995). Hertford: Hertfordshire County Council.

Hewett, S., Newson, J. and Newson, E. (1970) *The Family and the Handicapped Child*. London: George Allen and Unwin.

Hindmarch, C. (1993) *On the Death of a Child*. Oxford: Radcliffe Medical Press.

Hodgkinson, P. and Stewart, M. (1991) *Coping with Catastrophe – A Handbook of Disaster Management*. London: Routledge.

Holland, J. (1997) *Coping with Bereavement – a Handbook for Teachers*. Cardiff: Cardiff Academic Press.

Hornby, G. (1994) *Counselling in Child Disability*. London: Chapman and Hall.

Hornby, G. (1995) *Working with Parents of Children with Special Needs*. London: Cassell.

Hounslow, B., Stephenson, A., Stewart, J. and Crancher, J. (1982) *Children of Imprisoned Parents*. Sydney: Ministry of Youth and Community Services.

Howard League (1994) *The Voice of a Child: the impact on children of their maternal imprisonment*. London: Howard League.

Ihinger-Tallman, M. and Pasley, K. L. (1987) *Divorce and Re-marriage*. New York: Guildford Press.

James, I. A. (1995) 'Helping people with learning difficulties to cope with bereavement', *British Journal of Learning Disabilities* Vol. 23.

Jewett, C. (1982) *Helping Children Cope with Separation and Loss*. Boston: The Harvard Canman Press.

Judd, D. (1989) *Give Sorrow Words – working with a dying child*. London: Free Association Books.

Kasterbaum, R. (1997) *Death, Society and Human Experience* (2nd edn). St Louis: Mosby.

Kelly, J. (1988) 'Personal Communication – Adjustment in Children of Divorce', *Journal of Family Psychology* 2 (2) (Dec): 119–40.

Kinchin, D. (1998) *Post Traumatic Stress Disorder – the Invisible Injury*. Wantage: Success Unlimited.

Klein, M. (1960) *Our Adult World and its Roots in Infancy*. London: Tavistock Press.

Kloppel, D. A. and Hollins, S. (1989) 'Double Handicap: mental retardation and death in the family', *Death Studies*, **13**; 31–8.

Koochler, G. P. (1973) 'Children, death and cognitive development', in *British Journal of Medical Psychology*, **39**, 102–11.

Kronick, D. (1985) 'Dealing with death: Children's books and games', *Academic Theory* **20** (5), 627–33.

Kubler-Ross, E. (1983) *On Children and Death*. New York: Macmillan.

Lamb, B. and Layzell, S. (1993) *Disabled in Britain: A World Apart*. London: SCOPE.

Lansdown, R. and Goldman, A. (1988) 'The psychological care of children with malignant disease', *Journal of Child Psychology and Pyschiatry*, **29** (5), 555–67.

Larman, G. and Aungles, A. (1991) 'Children of prisoners and their outside carers: the invisible population', Paper at the 'Women and Law' Conference. London: Save the Children.

Leder, J. M. (1991) *Brothers and Sisters: How They Shape Our Lives*. New York: St Martin's Press.

Light, R. (1989) *Prisoners' Families*. Bristol: Bristol and Bath Centre for Criminal Justice.

Lindsay, W., Howells, L. and Pitcaithley, D. (1993) 'Cognitive therapy for depression with individuals with intellectual disabilities', *British Journal of Medical Psychology*, **66**, 135–41.

Lloyd, E. (1990) 'Prisoners' Families: a review of research to date'. Paper presented at the NACRO 'Silent Sentence Conference'. London: Save the Children.

Lloyd, E. (1995) *Children Visiting Holloway Prison: inside and outside perspectives on the all-day visits scheme at H.M.P. Holloway*. London: Save The Children.

McConkey, R. (1994) 'Early intervention: planning futures, shaping years', *Mental Handicap Research* **7** (1) 4–15.

McCown, D. E. (1984) 'Funeral attendance, cremation and young siblings', *Death Education*, **8**, 349–63.

McDermott, K. and King, R. (1992) 'Prison Rule 102 – Stand by your man: the impact of penal policy on the families of prisoners', in R. Shaw (ed.) *Prisoners' Children: what are the issues?* London: Routledge.

McEvoy, J. (1989) 'Investigating the concept of death in adults who are mentally handicapped', *British Journal of Subnormality* **35** (2), 115–21.

McLoughlin, I. (1986) 'Bereavement in the Mentally Handicapped', *British Journal of Hospital Medicine* **36**(4), 256–60.

McNeill, P. (1988), 'The Sociology of Health', in *New Statesman and Society*, July Edition.

Martinson, I. M., Gillis, C. and Colaizzo, D. C. (1990) 'Impact of Childhood Cancer on Healthy Siblings', *Cancer Nursing*, **13** (3), 183–90.

Matthews, J. (1983) *Forgotten Victims*. London: NACRO.

Maurer, A. (1961) 'The child's knowledge of non-existence', *Journal of Existentialist Psychiatry*, Vol. 2, 193–212.

Max, L. (1985) 'Parents' views of provisions, services and research', in Singh, N. and Wilton, K. M. (eds), *Mental Retardation in New Zealand*, Auckland: New Zealand Academic Studies Press, 250–62.

May, J. (1991) *Fathers of Children with Special Needs: New Horizons*. Bethesda: Association for the Care of Children's Health.

Mearns, D. and Thorne, B. (1988) *Person-Centred Counselling in Action*. London: SAGE.

Meyer, D. (1993) 'Lessons learned: cognitive coping strategies of overlooked family members', in A. Turnbull *et al. Cognitive Coping, Families and Disability*. Baltimore MD: Paul H Brookes.

Meyer, D. and Vadasy, P. (1986) *Grandparent Workshops*. Seattle, WA: University of Washington Press.

Meyer, D., and Vadasy, P. (1997) 'Meeting the unique concerns of brothers and sisters of children with special needs', in Carpenter, B. (ed.) *Families in Context: Emerging Trends in Family Support and Early Intervention*. London: David Fulton Publishers.

Minnes, P. M. (1988) 'Family stress associated with a developmentally handicapped child', in *International Review of Research in Mental Retardation* (ed. N. W. Bray) **15**, 195–226.

Mirfin-Veitch, B. and Bray, A. (1997) 'Grandparents: part of the family', in Carpenter, B. (1997) *Families in Context – Emerging Trends in Family Support and Early Intervention*. London: David Fulton Publishers.

Moddia, B. (1995) 'Grief Reactions and Learning Disabilities', *Nursing Standard* **9** (33), 38–9.

Monger, M. and Pendleton, J. (1981) 'Through care with prisoners' families', *Social Work Studies 3*: University of Nottingham.

Moody, R. and Moody, C. (1991) 'A family perspective – helping children acknowledge and express grief following death'. *Death Studies,* **15**, 587–602.

Moore, S. (1992) 'A link with normality: the role a school could play to help a prisoner's child in crisis', in Shaw, R. (ed.) *Prisoners' Children: What are the Issues?* London: Routledge.

Morris, P. (1967) 'Fathers in Prison', *British Journal of Criminology* **7**, 424.

Murgatroyd, S. and Woolfe, R. (1993) *Coping with Crisis: Understanding and Helping People in Need*. Buckingham: Open University.

Murphy, A. T. (1979) 'Members of the family: sisters and brothers of handicapped children', *Volta Review*, **81**, 352–62.

Murray, G. and Jampolsky, G. G. (eds) (1982) *Straight from the Siblings: Another Look at the Rainbow*. Berkeley CA: Celestial Arts.

NACRO (1993) *Women Leaving Prison*. London: NACRO.

NACRO (1994) *Prisoners' Families*. London: NACRO.

NACRO (1995) *Criminal Justice Digest*. London: NACRO.

Nord, K. (1989) 'Charting rough waters', *Family Therapy Networker* (Nov–Dec): 23–9.

Noy, S. (1991) *Stress Reactions*. Tel Aviv: Ministry of Defence.

O'Brien, T. (1998) *Promoting Positive Behaviour*. London: David Fulton Publishers.

Oldham Borough Council (1990) *Agreed Syllabus for Religious Education in Oldham*. Oldham Borough Council.

Olshansky, S. (1962) 'Chronic sorrow – a response to having a mentally defective child', in Younghusband, E. (ed.) *Social Work with Families*. London: George Allen and Unwin.

Oswin, M. (1981) *Bereavement and Mentally Handicapped People*. London: King's Fund Report KFC 81/234.

Oswin, M. (1991) *Am I Allowed to Cry? – A Study of Bereavement amongst People who have Learning Difficulties*. London: Souvenir Press.

Parke, R. D. (1986) 'Fathers, families and support systems', in Gallagher, J. and Vietze, P. M. (eds) *Research, Programs and Policy Issues*, Baltimore: Paul H. Brookes 101–13.

Parkes, C. M. (1972a) *Bereavement: Studies in Adult Life*. London: Sage.

Parkes, C. M. (1972b), 'Accuracy of predictions of survival in later stages of cancer', *British Medical Journal*, April 29–31.

Parkes, C. M. (1983) *Recovery from Bereavement*. New York: Basic Books.

Parkes, C. M. (1985) 'Bereavement', *British Journal of Psychiatry* **146**, 11–17.

Parkes, C., Relf, M. and Couldrick, A. (1996) *Counselling in Terminal Care and Bereavement*. Leicester: British Psychological Society.

Pellegrini, A. M. (1992a) *Coping with imprisonment on the outside: the perspectives of the children and their mothers*. Brunel University: unpublished thesis.

Pellegrini, A. M. (1992b), *Coping with a father in prison: the child's perspective*. Paper presented at the Fifth European Conference on Developmental Psychology, Seville.

Pennells, M., and Smith, S. (1995) *The Forgotten Mourners*. London: Jessica Kingsley.

Phillimore, P., Beattie, A. and Townsend, P. (1994) 'Widening Inequality in Northern England' (1981–1991), *British Medical Journal*, **308** (6937), 1125, 1128.

Piaget, J. (1951) *The Child's Conception of the World*. London: Routledge and Kegan Paul.

Pieper, E. (1976) 'Grandparents Can Help', *The Exceptional Parent*, April, 7–9.

Pope, V. (1987a), 'We all went to prison: the distress of prisoners' children', *Probation Journal*, September, 92–6.

Pope, V. (1987b) *We all went to prison: the distress of prisoners' children*, in Shaw, R. (1989) 'The health visitor and the prisoner's child', *Health Visitor* **62** (8), 248.

Posen, I. (1988) 'The Female Prison Population', in Morris, A. and Wilkinson, C. (eds) *Women and the Penal System*, Cropwood Conference, April 1998. Cambridge: Institution of Criminology.

Powell, T. H. and Gallagher, P. A. (1993) *Brothers and Sisters: A Special Part of Exceptional Families*, (2nd edn). Baltimore, MD: Paul H. Brookes.

Prickett, J. (ed.) (1980) *Death*. London: Lutterworth.

Ramsden, S. (1998) *Working with Children of Prisoners*. London: Save the Children.

Rando, T. A. (1985) 'Creating therapeutic rituals in the psychotherapy of the bereaved', *Psychotherapy*, **22**, 236–40.

Raphael, B. (1984) *The Anatomy of Bereavement: A Handbook for the Caring Professions*. London: Hutchinson.

Raphael, B. (1986) *When Disaster Strikes – A Handbook for the Caring Professions*. London: Unwin Hayman.

Report of consultative group on ministry among children (1995) *Unfinished Business: Children and the Churches*. London: CCBI Publications.

Richards, M. (1992) 'The separation of children and parents: some issues and problems', Shaw, R. (ed.) *Prisoners' Children: What are the Issues?* London: Routledge.

Richards, M., McWilliams, L., Allcock, L., Enterkin, J., Owens, P. and Woodrow, J. (1994) *The Family Ties of English Prisoners: the results of the Cambridge Project on Imprisonment and Family Ties*. Occasional Paper No 2. Cambridge: Centre for Family Research.

Rimmer, L. (1991) *Families in Focus*. London: Study Commission on the Family.

Robinson, M. (1991) *Family Transformation Through Divorce and Remarriage*. London: Routledge

Roos, P. (1978) 'Parents of mentally retarded children: misunderstood and mistreated', in Turnbull, H. T. and Turnbull, A. P. (eds) *Parents Speak Out*. Columbus: Charles Merell, 245–57.

Rotherham Metropolitan Borough Council (1989) *Agreed Syllabus for Religious Education*. Rotherham County Council.

Rowntree, J. (1998) *Foundations – Divorce and Separation: the Outcomes for Children*. York: Joseph Rowntree Foundation.

Rutter, J. (1994) *Refugee Children in the Classroom*. Stoke on Trent: Trentham Books.

Rutter, M. (1966) *Children of Sick Parents*. Oxford: Oxford University Press.

Sandler, A., Wareen, S. and Raver, S. (1995) 'Grandparents as a source of support for parents of children with disabilities: a brief report.' *Mental Retardation*, **3**, 248–9.

Saurkes, B. (1987) 'Siblings of the child with a life-threatening illness', *Journal of Children in Contemporary Society*, **19** (3/4), 159–84.

Save the Children (1997) *UN Convention on the Rights of the Child Training Pack*. London: Save the Children Alliance.

Savishinsky, J. S. (1990) *Dementia Sufferers and their Carers: A Study of Family Experiences and Supportive Services in the London Borough of Islington*. London: Polytechnic of North London.

SCAA (1994) *Model Syllabuses for Religious Education*. London: School Curriculum and Assessment Authority.

Segal, S. and Simkins, J. (1996) *Helping Children with Ill or Disabled Parents – a guide for Parents and Professionals*. London: Jessica Kingsley.

Seligman, M. and Darling, R. (1989) *Ordinary Families, Special Children*. New York: The Guildford Press.

Shaw, R. (1986) 'The Prevalence of Children of Imprisoned Fathers', *NASPO News* **6** (4).

Shaw, R. (1987) *Children of Imprisoned Fathers*. London: Hodder and Stoughton.

Shaw, R. (1989) Criminal justice and prisoners' children', in Light, R. (ed.) *Prisoners' Families*. Bristol: Bristol and Bath Centre for Criminal Justice.

Shaw, R. (ed.) (1992) *Prisoners' Children – What are the Issues?* London: Routledge.

Shulman, G. (1981) 'Divorce, single parenthood and stepfamilies: structural implications for these transactions', *International Journal of Family Therapy* (Summer) 87–112.

Simeonsson, R. J. and McHale, S. (1981) 'Review research and handicapped children: sibling relationships', *Child Care, Health and Development* **7**, 153–71.

Simos, B. G. (1979) *A Time to Grieve*. New York: Family Services Association.

Smith, S. C. and Pennells, M. (1995) (eds) *Interventions with Bereaved Children*. London: Jessica Kingsley.

Solnit, A. and Green, M. (1988) *Modern Perspectives in Child Development*. New York: Universities Press.

Sonnek, I. (1986) 'Grandparents and the extended family of handicapped children', in Fewell, R. and Vadasy, P. (eds) *Families of Handicapped Children*. Austin: Pro-Ed.

Speece, M. W. and Brent, S. W. (1984), 'Childrens' understanding of death: A review of three components of a death concept', *Child Development* **55**, 1671–86.

Spinetta, J. (1975) 'Communication patterns in families with life-threatening illness', in Sahler, U. (ed.) *The Child and Death*. St. Louis: Mosby.

Spinetta, J. (1984) 'Measurement of family function, communication and cultural effects', *Cancer* **53**, 2230–7.

Stannard, I. (1997) *The Puritan Way of Death: A Study in Religion, Culture and Social Change*. New York: Oxford University Press.

Stein, S. B. (1974) *About Dying: An Open Family Book for Parents and Children Together*. New York: Walker.

Stephenson, J. (1985) *Death, Grief and Mourning*. New York: The Free Press.

Strachan, J. (1981) 'Reactions to bereavement: a study of a group of hospital residents', *Apex* **9** (1), 20–1.

Stroebe, W. and Stroebe, M. (1987) *Bereavement and Health*. Cambridge: Cambridge University Press.

Tatelbaum, J. (1980) *The Courage to Grieve: Creative Living, Recovery and Growth Through Grief*. London: Cedar.

Terr, L. (1976) 'Children of Chowcilla – a study of psychic trauma', *Psychoanalytic Study of the Child*, **34**.

Thompson, C., Cole, D., Kammer, P. and Barker, R. (1984) 'Support groups for children of divorced parents', *Elementary School Guidance and Counselling* **19** (1) 88–9.

Trost, J. and Hultaker, O. (1983) 'Family in disaster', *International Journal of Mass Emergencies and Disasters* **1** (Special Edition).

Turner, J. and Graffam, J. (1987) 'Deceased loved ones in the dreams of mentally retarded adults', *American Journal of Retardation*, **92**, 282–9.

Tyhurst, L. (1977) 'Psychosocial First Aid for refugees', *Mental Health in Society* **4**, 319–43.

Vadasy, P. F., Fewell, R. R. and Meyer, D. J. (1986) 'Grandparents of Children with Special Needs: Insights into their experiences and concerns', *Journal of the Division of Early Childhood* **10** (1), 36–44.

Valente, S., Saunders, J. and Street, R. (1988) 'Adolescent bereavement following suicide: an examination of relevant literature', *Journal of Counselling and Development*, **67**, 174–7.

Vander-Wyden, P. (1991) *Butterflies – Talking with Children about Death and Life Eternal*. Texas: Tarbor.

Van Eerdewegh, M., Bieri, M., Parrilla, R. and Clayton, P. (1985) 'The Bereaved Child', *British Journal of Psychiatry*, **140**, 23–9.

Vernick, J. (1973) 'Meaningful communication with the fatally ill child', in Anthony, E. and Koupernick, E. (eds) *The Child and his Family*, **11**, New York: Wiley.

Visher, E. and Visher, J. (1988) *Stepfamilies: – a Guide to Working with Stepparents and Children*. New York: Bruner Mazel.

Waechter, E. (1971) *Death Anxiety in Children with Fatal Illness*. Unpublished thesis, Washington.

Walczak, Y. and Burns, S. (1984) *Divorce: the Child's Point of View*. London: Harper and Row.

Wald, E. (1981) *The Remarried Family: Change and Promise*. New York: Families Association of America.

Wallerstein, J. and Blakeslee, S. (1989) *Second Chances: Men, Women and Children a Decade after Divorce*. London: Bantam Press.

Webb, S. (1994) *Troubled and Vulnerable Children: A Practical Guide for Heads*. Kingston upon Thames: Croner Publications.

Weiss, R. (1975) *Marital Separation: Coping with the end of marriage and the transition to being single again*. New York: Basic Books.

Weller, E. B., Weller, R. A., Fristad, M. A., Cain, S. E. and Bowes, J. M. (1988) 'Should Children Attend their Parents' Funeral?' *Journal of American Academy of Child and Adolescent Psychiatry* **27**, 559–62.

Wenestam, C. G. (1982) *Children's Reactions to the Word 'Death'*. Gotenborg: Department of Education, Gotenborg University.

White, S. (1989) 'Mothers in custody and the punishment of children', in *Probation Journal* **36** (3), 106–9.

Wilkinson, C. (1998) 'The post-release experience of women prisoners', in Morris, A. and Wilkinson, C. (eds) *Women and the Penal System*. Cropwood Conference Series 19. Cambridge: Institute of Criminology.

Woodrow, J. (1992) 'Mothers Inside, Children Outside', in Shaw, R. (ed.) (1992) *Prisoners' Children: What are the Issues?* London: Routledge.

Worden, J. W. (1988) *Grief Counselling and Grief Therapy*. London: Routledge.

Yule, W. and Gold, A. (1993) *Wise Before the Event – Coping with Crises in Schools*. London: Colouste Gulbenkian Foundation.

Index

DATE DUE

			Printed in USA

Loss, Change and Grief

An Educational Perspective

Erica Brown

Helping children come to terms with and be aware of loss, change and grief is an undeveloped area within education although they are universal features of human experience. Here the author fosters a positive attitude to teaching and learning about such issues. She explores many experiences of loss and grief and different beliefs and practices are discussed so that the reader can gain a better understanding of how children grieve. She also provides suggestions for ways in which this topic can be taught within the school curriculum and offers practical suggestions for effective, professional collaboration.

The Author

Erica Brown *is Head of Research and Development (Special Educational Needs) at Westminster College in Oxford.*

Other titles of interest

Counselling and Guidance in Schools
Developing Policy and Practice
Colleen McLaughlin, Pam Clark
and Meryl Chisholm
1-85346-423-6

Counselling
Approaches and Issues in Education
Helen Cowie and Andrea Pecherek
1-85346-293-4

Peer Counselling in Schools
A Time to Listen
Edited by Helen Cowie and Sonia Sharp
1-85346-367-1

Spiritual, Moral, Social and Cultural Education
Policy, Practice and Values
Edited by Stephen Bigger and Erica Brown
1-85346-593-3

Individual Counselling Theory and Practice
A Reference Guide
Doula Nicolson and Harry Ayers
1-85346-373-6

RE for All
Erica Brown
1-85346-392-2

Families in Context
Emerging Trends in Family Support and
Early Intervention
Edited by Barry Carpenter
1-85346-489-9

David Fulton Publishers

London

ISBN 1-85346-465-1

9 781853 464652